Creative Quilts
Inspiration, Texture and Stitch

Sandra Meech

BATSFORD

Acknowledgements

I would like to thank friends and colleagues for their contribution to this book, especially the members of Quilt Art who are always a great support to me, Annette Collinge, for making available her textile collection, and Michael Wicks for his excellent photography. Above all, I would like to thank my family, who have constantly encouraged my artistic endeavours over the years.

First published in the United Kingdom in 2006 by
Batsford
151 Freston Road
London
W10 6TH

An imprint of Anova Books Company Ltd

ISBN 0 7134 9006 3
ISBN (13-digit) 9780713490060

A CIP catalogue record for this book is available from the British Library.

10 9 8 7 6 5 4 3 2 1

Reproduction by Anorax Imaging, Leeds, UK
Printed and bound by CT Printing Ltd, China

This book can be ordered direct from the publisher at the website:
www.anovabooks.com
Or try your local bookshop

Page 1: **Within 4 Walls** *(Sandra Meech).*

Page 2: **Lille Wall** *(detail) (Sandra Meech).*

Page 3: **Acid Rain** *(Sandra Meech).*

Left: **Cup and Ring (Kilmartin)** *(Sandra Meech).*

Contents

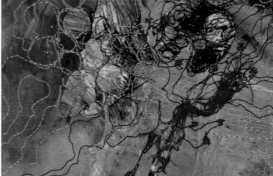

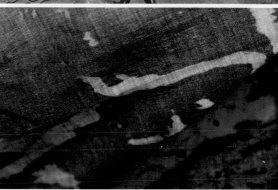

Using this book

Creativity may sometimes seem elusive, but however hard it may seem to find, it is most certainly within everyone's grasp. Each individual comes to contemporary quilting from a unique background; some have a wealth of stitch experience, while others may have training in art and design. Even for the most experienced, the challenge of exploring new ideas for the next project can be daunting. The aim of this 'self-study guide' is to examine the process of finding your own creativity and introduce exercises to consolidate these skills in order to build confidence. The quilter or textile student who has acquired the basics of piecing and stitch techniques can dip into the variety of short workshops and classes on offer in order to organize new ideas on personal themes that may be explored in future work. Sometimes old methods don't work any more – you might be in the doldrums in your textile work and finding inspiration seems impossible. If so, it is time to rejuvenate your creative approach and find new and different ways to move forward. Freeing your mind to consider new pathways is part of this creative journey.

Throughout this book the main focus of inspiration will be the world around us, encompassing art, architecture, industry and urban living as well as the cultures and textiles of various peoples, with the addition of ecological and family themes. Throughout each chapter there will be suggestions for you to try. With subjects ranging from mind mapping and other simple brainstorming exercises in the first chapter, the pace is set for inspiration in the following chapter. Next, taking inspiration from man's endeavours in the world around us, we will consider modern artists whose works may guide us. No inspirational book can work without a review of colour and composition or revisiting the elements and principles of design.

One of the most important steps in this journey is documenting information in a sketchbook, and Chapter 4 is dedicated to this subject. Working through the different techniques, each student will practise a method of working that will see them through many different themes in future textile work. Texture in the world of contemporary quilt art is introduced, and three-dimensional considerations are explored. New techniques are included with a design class on the use of Wireform (see page 96).

Hopefully you will find this book to be a valuable reference for every new project. There is an emphasis on world textiles as a theme to develop, and many surface design, dyeing and embellishment considerations as well as new stitch possibilities are considered. We should all strive to achieve a level of professionalism in our quilt art and stitched textiles, so a final chapter on working in series, exhibiting and promoting yourself offers an important key to realizing your future ambitions.

Use this workbook to help you to find and develop your own ideas – it is full of exciting works by leading quilt and textile artists from around the world and illustrated with helpful pictures and diagrams. Above all, use this book with a sense of adventure and added confidence, as you find exciting new ways to make creative quilts.

Left: **Inuit Girl** *(Sandra Meech) Silk-screen print.*

Right: **Ice Blue** *(Sandra Meech) Painted and textured paper collage showing melting glaciers.*

Top: **Near North Algonquin** *(Sandra Meech) Ontario lakes and woodlands at different stages of growth. Photo imagery with paint and stitch. Above:* **Woodland sketchbook** *(Sandra Meech). Sketchbook with printed paper and magazine collage showing the rise and fall of water levels.*

Chapter One
Exploring Creativity

There are many different ways in which to explore our own unique creative potential in the stitched textiles we make. Some of these approaches are simple and straightforward; others are a journey of discovery on a personal theme.

We all come to contemporary quilt making from different backgrounds and life experience and it is this richness that we need to celebrate. Some tap into the creative process as teachers; some through hobbies such as dressmaking, soft furnishing, weaving or embroidery, and some express themselves in planning a garden or in interior decorating. Others, who are perhaps art trained or have a graphic or design background, discover a need to express themselves with stitch marks and textures instead of paint. Some, trained in more disciplined professions such as mathematics or science, come into textiles to experience the freedom of expression in contemporary quilt art. However, very few successful contemporary quilt artists can just begin a new work once they have an idea in mind. They will need to work through their own creative process of organizing thoughts and ideas that eventually will culminate in a new and interesting piece. You'll find suggestions on how to do this in this book.

Some have a natural talent for art and can easily make good design and colour choices, while others have to learn and work at these skills constantly. By understanding the principles and elements of design and constantly practising the rules of composition and colour, it is possible to gain greater confidence in the creative process.

In this first chapter we will be exploring this creative process, from beginning the journey by getting started with a simple plan. We will then begin to explore techniques for stimulating creativity, from mind-map brainstorming to collecting information, writings and photographs in a journal or sketchbook and looking at simple artistic approaches with line and pattern plus practical design rules.

**'Creativity requires the courage to let go of certainties.
Conditions for creativity are: to be puzzled, to concentrate, to accept conflict and
tension, to be born everyday, to feel a sense of self'**
Erich Fromme

Above: **Lille Wall** *(Sandra Meech). This original poster inspired many digital effects.*

Getting started

Getting started may be the hardest part of the whole process, but once a decision has been made that it is time to 'bite the bullet' and begin the adventure it will never again seem so daunting. A positive mental attitude is crucial.

Getting your teeth into an inspiring theme is key to getting started. Helpful practices include keeping a notebook handy for ideas and observations, collecting newspaper or magazine articles that interest you, and carrying a digital camera with you. Turning these practices into habits will help you to look at the world with fresh eyes.

Ideally, you will have a place to work – somewhere that has a pinboard on which you can collect and view all the interesting information you have gathered on your travels. This collection could include fabric swatches and photo or postcard details of fibre-art pieces that inspire. Don't confine yourself to textiles – look at paintings, sculpture, collectibles, interiors, garden design or anything else that can feed your creative journey.

The following good habits are all part of the creative process:

➤ *Keep a notebook – document ideas, diary writings, emotional reactions, descriptions.*

➤ *Collect magazine and newspaper articles.*

➤ *Take quick and easy digital photos.*

➤ *Use a pinboard for collecting information, fabrics, photos or anything else that might inspire you.*

➤ *Visit exhibitions, but don't confine yourself to textiles – look at museum collections, art, architecture, gardens and sculpture.*

➤ *Make a file of new techniques or surface-design methods that you have learned in workshops and include the samples you have made for reference, adding others you would like to try.*

Left: **Making the World a Safer Place** *(Susan Denton, UK). The second in a triptych about the invasion of Iraq.*

A theme to inspire

Where do we find the theme that will captivate us? Now is the time to look closely at the world around you. As you do, wonderful themes will appear. Whether these are based on art and architecture, nature in the landscape, or man and his environment (textiles, culture, myth or tradition), you will always have an immediate emotional and personal response to the subject. There are so many choices of theme, but there will always be one that you keep returning to, something that 'pops up' in your thoughts and won't go away.

The best way forward is to combine personal experience with added research (the internet, newspaper or magazine articles). You will bring much of yourself to the experience and this will definitely be reflected positively in your work. Inspiration can come in so many different ways: through visiting an exotic place, learning about the textiles, traditions and history of different cultures or from everyday life. Look, for example, at the architecture and artefacts around you, both old and new. You might find beauty in the colours and textures of derelict, decaying walls or rusted farm implements, or even in the designs of modern inventions.

Throughout this book, the focus is mainly on themes that have been directly influenced by man and the environment and less on the natural world, but if your instinct leads you towards the latter, follow it.

Above: **Stills from a Life Series #6** *(Dominie Nash, USA). Familiar objects in a new context – as a still-life composition with interesting shapes and patterns that become abstract as they interact with each other.*

Subjects that reflect human endeavour, positive and negative, could include the following:

➤ *Periods of painting, other art forms and architecture, old and new.*

➤ *Costume, clothing, world textiles and sewing traditions.*

➤ *Symbolism, mythical stories, religions.*

➤ *Industry, cityscapes, tall buildings, reflections in glass and metal.*

➤ *Issues associated with urban living, such as overcrowded spaces or homelessness.*

➤ *Pollution, global warming, environmental or other political issues.*

➤ *Details such as the decaying paintwork on a building, rusting iron, torn poster messages or colourful graffiti.*

➤ *Collections, perhaps of toys, shoes or jewellery.*

➤ *Personal themes, which may also reflect deeper emotions and feelings, offering a way to cope with health problems, illness, memory loss or social crisis.*

A theme has hidden depth

Every chosen idea may be developed through at least three conceptual layers. The top level deals with the outward appearance of the piece – the design, colour choice, materials and sewing techniques. This is the most important layer, as it is the level at which the textile is viewed. The stitch and embellishment choices are important at this stage, and should be true to the integrity of the theme. The middle level reflects the deeper meaning of the subject – a more subtle interpretation that could include hidden issues or meanings not always immediately apparent. Underlying these and perhaps the least obvious could be an emotional reaction to the theme, one that could subtly impact your colour or stitch choices.

We now have to consider how we are going to develop our theme further.

Far left: **Creation of Woman: Venus** *(Susan Chapman, UK). This piece was inspired by the sculptural form and the role of women in society. Left:* **Layers of Inspiration** *(Sandra Meech). This piece has three conceptual layers: its outward appearance (colour, design and stitch), the deeper meaning of the subject, and finally my own personal and emotional response to it.*

Mind maps and brainstorming ideas

Mind maps and other brainstorming methods have been used in business for years. Students in school learn these techniques for associating and connecting words and ideas in order to help them organize thoughts for studying, essays and revision. You can also use the mind-map formula to focus on ideas as you plan your next creative project. Visualizing all aspects of that theme on paper and showing how different facets relate and connect to each other will strengthen and consolidate the visual impact and meaning of your work.

Above: **New Dawn** *(Sandra Meech). This piece was inspired by the Berlin Wall coming down in 1989, heralding a new future for many. Photo images of graffiti-painted papers.*

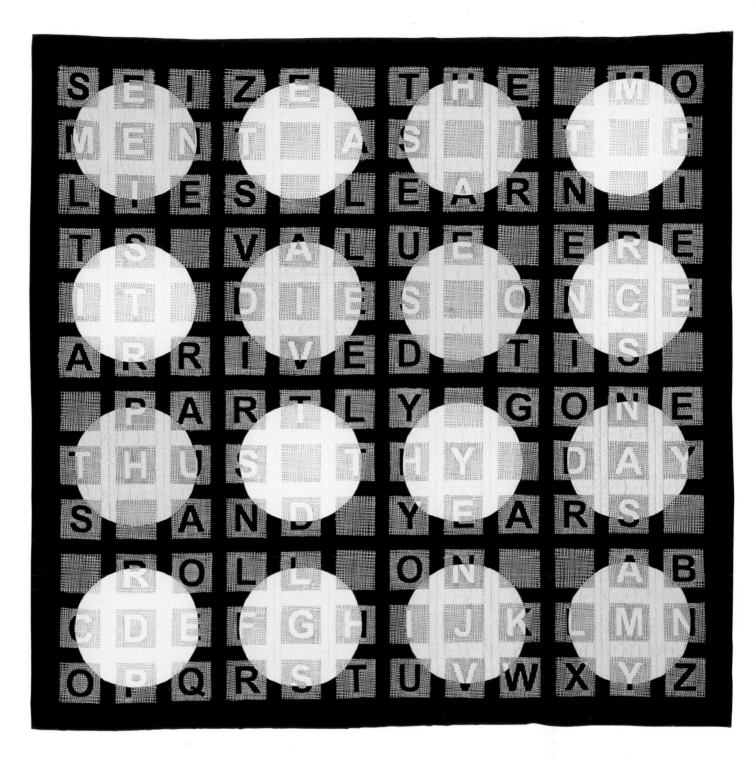

So what is 'mind mapping'? It is a logical progression that helps to organize and control our thoughts while we visualize them with words in a graphic way. This raises the level of understanding we have on our theme, allowing us also to explore some deeper issues. By using this 'radiant thinking' plan, mapped out like the spokes of a wheel, the central theme is highlighted and ideas, words and thoughts about it radiate outwards. Sometimes they continue to develop in one direction and other times they connect with each other.

Above: **Sampler Quilt** *(Sarah Impey, UK). 'Seize the moment as it flies, learn its value ere it dies…' Words inspired this beautiful machine-stitched art quilt. Opposite page:* **Without Words** *(Sandra Meech). Layers of hidden words through sheers with added copper elements.*

Questions to ask include the following:

➤ *What is my theme? If you feel passionate or intensely interested in a subject, you will enjoy collecting information, taking photos, exploring new techniques or exchanging views.*

➤ *How would I describe this subject in words? Adjectives – smooth, gentle, vibrant, energetic or angry, for example – could also inspire pattern and shape that reflects the subject. Use a thesaurus to collect words.*

➤ *Do I have emotions, feelings or an experience relating to the theme? Quick-fire word lists could revisit a moment in time or a place that has been forgotten about.*

➤ *How important is colour? Is there a strong design element that comes to mind? Colour will be obvious right from the start, and so, sometimes, are design decisions.*

➤ *Are there historical or cultural aspects related to my theme? Tradition, myths, stories or ancient symbols could certainly provide 'hidden depth' to your work.*

➤ *How has man affected this theme in both positive and negative ways?*

➤ *What kind of textures, surfaces, stitch or related fibre disciplines come to mind? Are there other disciplines, such as weaving, felt-making or techniques with metal, ceramics, glass or wood, that could contribute to the theme?*

➤ *What stitch techniques could make the textile more dynamic?*
If you use mind maps at the beginning of the creative journey you will reap rich benefits. With the help of this mental tool, we can explore all creative possibilities, anywhere, anytime, as we clear our mind of assumptions about a subject by looking in depth at all the angles. Using mind maps, we can create an immediate result or a crucial change in thinking. By organizing ourselves this way, we can make informed design, colour, surface and stitch decisions. A mind map also allows us to capture flashes of insight – the spark of an idea as it happens. Mind maps become the visual overview of all the possibilities ahead of us in our project, making it easier to plan creatively in the future. Practise them often, so they become easier.

Above: **Broken Windows** *(Bente Vold Klausen, Norway). Painted, dyed and printed fabrics are evocative of abandoned industrial buildings.*

Opposite page: **In Retreat** *(Sandra Meech). This quilt was inspired by global warming in the Arctic.*

Creativity plus – creating a personal mind map

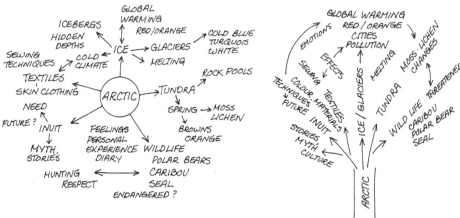

Above: Mind map with an Arctic theme.

To create your own mind map, all you need to do is to follow this simple process:

➤ *On a sheet of white paper begin with your theme in large letters in the centre.*

➤ *Give yourself at least five different tangents radiating out from the centre (more may be added later). Remind yourself of descriptive words, emotional feelings and observations. Ask how humanity is involved. Check whether there are negative influences to address. Consider the surface fabric techniques that might be explored. The considerations involved will entirely depend on your theme, but it is important to spotlight all the different aspects or issues involved.*

➤ *From these tangents, other ideas will pop up and as this happens it is good to look again at what is forming, noticing that one or two of the ideas connect.*

➤ *Another approach is to consider this quest as a journey along a path, with the different tangents radiating out.*

➤ *Mind maps can be created anywhere, so always travel with a notebook and pen.*

➤ *Little sketches could be included, indicating colour or referring to photographs or articles collected.*

To see how varied and personal mind maps can be, try this exercise with some friends, all sharing the same theme. You may be surprised at how different the results will be. Remember, however, that in general a mind map is your own personal research and is not for public scrutiny. It should include anything that pops into your mind. The end result may look like a jumble but it could be a valuable first step in the creative process.

'The best way to have a good idea is to get lots of ideas.'

Linus Pauling

*Above: **Torn Poster, Newcastle** (Sandra Meech). Photograph showing connected words and symbols in peeling layers.*

*Opposite page, left: **Inuit sketchbook** (Sandra Meech). Painted pages and a portrait, include fabrics, plastics and stitch.*

*Opposite page, right: **Algonquin Passage** (detail) (Sandra Meech). Ghostly trees contrast with colour images in a piece inspired by the cycles of nature.*

Keeping journals and sketchbooks

Gathering information is always a first step in discovering and developing a theme. Taking photo images and noting down personal descriptions and observations is the best way to get started. Remember that these sketchbook journals are personal and not meant to be seen by anyone (see pages 66–81). Sketch and stitch books from start to finish will be covered in greater detail in Chapter 3, but for now it is important to note that your personal journal/sketchbook is the place in which to include some or all of the following elements:

➤ *Personal thoughts, ideas and drawings, magazine or newspaper cuttings, research material, photos and any memorabilia that will strengthen your understanding of the subject, inspiring the creative process and indicating steps that might need to be documented.*

➤ *Mixed-media and surface collage that could become a starting point for fabric composition.*

➤ *Sketches and drawings – although personal and simple, these can inspire further design decisions.*

➤ *Colour experiments and samples of colour choices.*

➤ *Explorations in composition, which at this stage can be valuable tools for developing and consolidating designs for a new textile piece.*

➤ *An overview of different ideas, words of inspiration and a 'plan of attack'.*

➤ *Experimental fabric pages, which can include mark-making stitches, with additional fabrics for variety.*

A sketchbook or journal is the ideal way to consolidate all the creative approaches you may use in order to begin that next important creative quilt or stitched textile.

Design class – Drawing for design

'Help! I can't draw ...'

Drawing in line needn't be a daunting prospect. Turning ideas into sketches, drawings or shapes is the beginning of a personal journey. The more you practise, the easier it will become. Armed with basic art supplies, an open mind and some backup photographic support, you will be surprised at how much can be achieved.

Exercise 1 Drawing with words

This exercise could inspire the design and colour of new work, and also consolidate stitch 'marks' to be added at the quilting stage. The quicker and more intuitively you work, the more dynamic the marks will be.

1. Choose from the following words. Spending no longer than 10 seconds on each, take a pen or coloured pencil, close your eyes and 'draw' the word (see picture below).

   ANGER JOY CONFUSED COLD HOT SAD LOVE FEAR CROWDED FREEDOM SOFT HARD JAGGED SMOOTH ROUGH LIVELY SOMBRE

2. Choose some of your own words and have fun with the creative process.

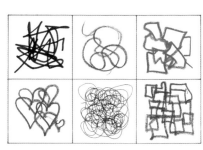

Exercise 2 Drawing with line

Consider this a liberating warm-up exercise.

1. Draw an object by making a continuous line in black pen, focusing on the object, not on your paper. See how expressive your line can be. See picture, right.

2. Next, again with a continuous line, draw the same object with the hand you do not usually write with (this time you can look). See picture, below right.

The result should be free and quite abstract, providing an interesting starting point from which to develop further. You might, for example, consider the following developments:

➤ *Enlarge a section on a photocopier, making several copies.*

➤ *Use oil pastels as a resist and then apply a wash of paint or add marks with coloured pencils. See picture, left.*

Materials for all exercises

Before you begin, assemble the following materials:

➤ White letterhead paper (alternatively, use a cartridge sketchbook), tracing paper, thin layout and squared paper

➤ Fine and thick black pens, soft (4B) pencils and set of 24 coloured pencils

➤ Oil pastels and paints for coloured washes – use inks, watercolours or Brusho paints for washes

➤ Glue stick or spray adhesive (use sparingly and in a well-ventilated room)

➤ Any photographs or pictures of still-life objects as reference

➤ Two 'L' s cut from thin card to create window apertures (there is more about using 'windows' on page 58)

Exercise 3 Drawing shapes

This next exercise could be the most valuable of the three, and you might even use it to inspire a series of work. Here, shapes are layered together to form abstracted contemporary designs. Choose a subject with a simple shape to start with, and draw it. Think about Picasso, Miró, Braque or Matisse and remember how they composed everyday objects in a creative way.

1. Draw an outline of the subject as a master copy (fig a).

2. Rotate the object by 45 degrees and draw it again, then at a 90-degree angle. With tracing paper, record the first three outlines and turn them over to form mirror images. These can be layered and drawn again for variety (fig b).

3. Consider the negative space (the space around the object). Use cross-hatched or parallel lines, either drawn in pen or with soft pencil to give grey tones (fig c).

4. With a repeated or overlay design (fig d), take an interesting detail (figs e, f and g).

5. Practise counter change (reversing black to white) with an overlay design and fill in black-and-white shapes (fig h).

6. Use squared paper and tracings to start imposing a series of borders on a layered design (fig i), incorporating counter change methods in colour (fig j). Keep a sample in line as a master copy.

Also illustrated are two examples of the wonderful effects that can be created with Photoshop Elements by scanning the master copy into the computer and applying colour. Experiments of this type can be great fun (figs k and l). Remember to keep all design examples in a file for future reference.

i.

j.

k.

l.

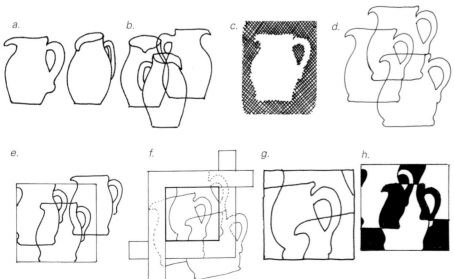

a.

b.

c.

d.

e.

f.

g.

h.

ChapterTwo
Themes to Inspire

Early exposure to quiltmaking or embroidery is usually restricted to traditional techniques. A novice quilter will learn historic block patterns or designs from books first and, although these may prove quite satisfying, may yearn to create a contemporary quilt that is unique and original. The question then is 'Where do I start?' Nature and the world around us are great places to find inspiration, but in this book the inspirational source on which I would like to focus is man's impact on the world around us.

Be willing to try something different – something you haven't tried before – and take chances!

Nature and the environment

From spring flowers in the garden to a wonderful sunset by the sea, blue skies, mountains or the colours of the desert, we can find immediate pleasure in nature. As the original source for perfect colour and design choices, nature can also bring dual meanings, evoking an emotional response. For example, rather than simply celebrating the detail of a flower in a contemporary quilt, it might be more interesting to look at its significance and history in different cultures. Has it religious, historical or mythical connotations, and do these vary from culture to culture? White flowers in the western world symbolize purity, virginity and truth, but in Eastern cultures they represent death.

Above: Textiles from Rajasthan in northern India. Fabric and stitch disciplines from around the world can inspire future work.
Left: **London Skyline** *(Sandra Meech). Urban cityscapes with their historical and modern buildings can provide powerful themes for contemporary quilts.*
Right: **Inuit textile basket** *(Sandra Meech). This is a constructed textile with a design taken from a Japanese 'pinwheel'-shaped bag. Applied images were then bonded and stitched onto the heavy interfacing.*

Above: **Protected** *(Sandra Meech).*
Photographic panorama.

Above: *Wooden textile stamps can create
unique fabric on hand-dyed cotton.*

Above: *Kuba cloth. African raffia-fibre cloth is
patched and applied with a bold textile design.*

Ecological issues can be thought-provoking: my own interest in the Arctic landscape evokes cold, hard, imagery of this barren landscape with blues, white and turquoise. But with current concerns about global warming and evidence that this may be raising temperatures and affecting nature's delicate balance, I have begun to include cityscapes, and warm colours in a cold palette to illustrate this.

Natural disasters, such as the years of drought in Ethiopia, the tsunami in Asia or the increased frequency of hurricanes bring us closer to others who are suffering. Quilters and embroiderers, whether in groups or as individuals, may respond by working through emotive themes, often raising significant amounts of money to help a cause.

Man's impact on the landscape, from formal garden design to rotated crops, elegant wind turbines or stone walls, may provide inspiration. Ley lines, crop circles or aerial views illustrate the patchwork of line and shape in the landscape and topographic maps will provide contours, symbols, pattern and shapes to inspire quilt lines and stitch marks.

You might consider some of the following options:

➤ *Use colour photocopies or painted papers for collage, combining two themes – the natural world and textile detail.*

➤ *Take two different sources, this time using a symbol or shape in the theme: for example, a spiral shape cut out of a city landscape, offering two themes in one design.*

➤ *Experiment with digital images taken from Photoshop Elements or Paintshop Pro. This can have interesting results as subtle colours in nature take on dynamic proportions, and the experiment could be a starting point for creative new work.*

World textiles

Textiles through the ages and in all parts of the world have been influenced by people and their environment. Early man decorated his bone tools and left a glimpse of his life in drawings on cave walls. The marks we make today are as important to us as they were to our ancestors, offering an insight into the way we observe the world and our emotional reaction to it. Many designs and symbols have appeared simultaneously in different parts of the world in different cultures: the spiral designs featured on ancient floor tiles, symbolic of evolution and the cycle of life, are a wonderful example of this. Even today in stitched textiles, 'what goes around, comes around'.

You may have your own ideas about incorporating old and new themes, but you might like to consider experimenting with some of the following ideas:

➤ *Investigate an ancient symbol and its meaning (the internet and Dover publications are great sources).*

➤ *Make a stamp of a spiral shape or another shape in your theme and, using metallic fabric paint, overprint your shape on hand-dyed or batik fabric. Stamps and blocks come in all forms, ranging from wood blocks to commercial designs. The best type to use are the ones you have made yourself.*

➤ *Use discharge or dilute bleach to take away colour (fabric will need to be treated before use).*

Textiles, from past to present

Traditional designs, sewing techniques, and dyeing and printing methods are still practised today. We can tap into these skills in our more contemporary work. Textiles from many regions of the world illustrate that similar techniques have been developed at different places and at different times, styles of weaving, dyeing cloth and embroidery emerging in varying forms in separate cultures. This brief reference is a simple overview of world textiles. Nevertheless, it shows the influences of ancient traditions on the design and sewing methods we use today.

Early materials

From the earliest times, man used skins and hide for clothing, decorated with images of daily life. In time, wool and hair became felt and yarn. Cotton was developed in India and silk in China, and both were traded to the west along the Silk Route. Tree bark and leaf fibres were used to make cloth and raffia in Africa, North America and Polynesia.

Today, many of these same fibres and patterns find their way into contemporary textiles, plastic, metal, paper, wood and acrylic being combined with a wide mix of fabrics, including sheers, nets, woven designs, metallic fabrics and surfaces that also incorporate photo imagery.

Hand-worked fibre surfaces

Early cultures evolved techniques of looping, knotting, interlacing and twining fibres together. Knitting originally developed in Egyptian times, when fibres as diverse as wool from sheep, goats or alpaca were used. In China and New Guinea, netting, looping and linking of fibres created bags of a type still made today. Another discipline, crochet, also became popular, worked in wool, cotton or silk.

Lace making, macramé and braiding have also influenced the contemporary stitched textiles we see today. For your next project, therefore, you might like to consider incorporating a traditional craft technique that you haven't used before.

Above: Mola is a reverse-appliqué sewing technique from the San Blas islands in Central America.

Above: African indigo-dyed woven and embroidered textiles are very contemporary in design.

Above: Inuit lino-cut images bleached out of dyed paper and painted with screen inks. (Sandra Meech).

Woven fabrics

Every part of the world, from the Arctic and Scandinavia to Africa, has a history of woven textiles that are rich in pattern, with strong detail and intense colours unique to each region. Some fabrics were heavy, for warmth and protection; others, such as lightweight calicoes and muslins, were designed for hot climates, while some even-weave types evolved as a background for counted thread embroidery. Woven fabrics include plain weaves, twill, tapestry, warp- and weft-faced types, strip and double weaves, damask, brocade and velvet. Today many quilting fabric patterns are inspired by themes found in world textiles, such as African geometric patterns, Chinese brocades or Navaho Indian designs. Try using a traditional woven pattern or the detail in a modern commercial print as a theme for a contemporary piece.

Fabric painting and printing

Decoration and detail representing nature, religion or traditional stories, coloured with natural pigments, have been used for centuries. From Native American hide paintings to the daubed 'mud cloth' textiles of Mali, man has always 'made his mark' on ceremonial fabrics. Woodblock printing methods, first developed in China, are still a popular method of adding pattern to a cloth surface. Multi-coloured block prints from India and stencilled or silk-screen fabrics from Japan are still exported around the world and are often seen in contemporary quilts. Creating surfaces for today's quilts often entails a journey back to basic traditional methods and techniques, though perhaps with a modern slant. The addition of metallic paints, foils and oil-based mark-making sticks also provides new ways to decorate cloth.

Left: **Art Cloth 1** *(Els van Baarle, Netherlands). Batik on silk with hand-painted motifs.*

Above: **Art Cloth 2** *(Els van Baarle, Netherlands) Batik on silk.*

Above: **Crazy (detail)** *(Sandra Meech). A modern crazy patchwork sampler makes a personal statement.*

Dyed fabrics

A subject of great interest for today's quilter, dyeing fabric ensures a longer fabric design life than painting and printing methods, as all the fibres are immersed in the dye. Natural dyes have always been popular. From Ancient Egypt came indigo dyeing methods, and the basic techniques are still practised today in many parts of the world, notably Indonesia, Africa, India, China and Japan. Tie-dye methods also originated in this part of the world and are now popular in the West. Aligned with this are stitch-resist techniques, which can provide wonderful patterning across the fabric surface. Batik, a wax-resist technique from early China, is now very popular. In the 20th century, commercial dyes such as Procion became popular, providing home textile artists with the facility to create their own coloured fabrics. At the same time, modern commercial prints provide quilters with vibrant contemporary fabric.

Patchwork and quilting traditions

Patchwork, or piecework, refers to pieces of fabrics that are sewn together, often in a geometric pattern. Very early samples included silks and pattered fabrics from the East that were made into decorative coverlets in Europe. During the 1800s, piecing recycled fabrics became a more utilitarian and practical way of making warm bed coverings.

Non-block piecing consists of shaped pieces of fabric that are often sewn over a paper template and stitched together by hand. Designs include hexagons, clamshell patterns, drunkard's path, strip piecing, rail fence, log cabin and double wedding ring designs. Many patterns have their origins in England and Europe. Victorian 'crazy' piecing falls into a category of its own, with a variety of luscious fabrics such as silk, velvet, sateen, wool and cotton randomly combined and elaborately embellished with embroidery stitches.

Block-piecing patterns were developed in North America, where recycled fabrics were used to make practical warm quilts. Today, patterns abound and thousands of block patterns are on offer. Piecing with standard 6mm (¼in) seams became much faster with the advent of the sewing machine. Today's quilter can use both hand and machine methods.

Contemporary piecing styles

The use of rotary cutting methods, specialist plastic templates and rulers offers many new techniques to help and inspire the quilter. Curves and creative, abstract strip-piecing techniques are evolving, often combined with painted and dyed surfaces that include a mix of media. In this way, the traditional quilt has been transformed. Today, sheers, photo imagery, paper, plastics and metal can reflect art-quilt themes as they never have before.

Appliqué

In many cultures, appliqué started as the practical 'patching' of damaged material, later becoming an art form on its own. Motifs had religious significance or were symbols of rank and importance. As early as 980 BC, in Egypt, appliqué was used in funeral decoration. Today, many forms of appliqué offer a popular way of giving colour, design and dimension to a background fabric.

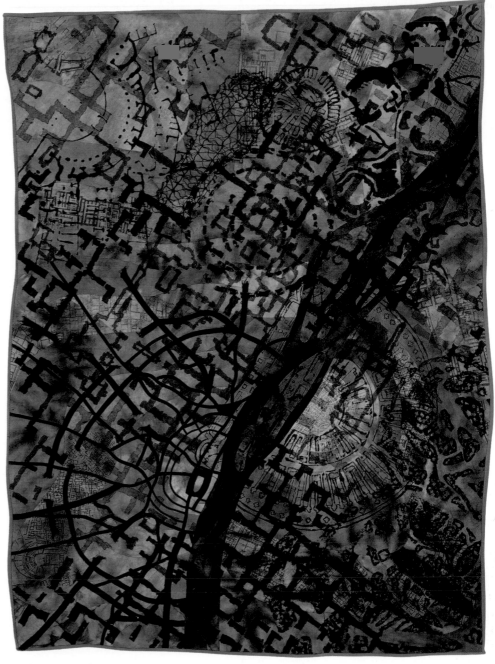

Above: **Layers** *(Eszter Bornemisza, Hungary). This piece is inspired by old maps of Budapest and imprints of former settlements.*

Early traditions An early 16th-century style of appliqué, *broderie perse*, included motifs (birds, trees, animals and flowers) taken from Indian printed chintz fabrics. These were cut out and applied to a background fabric. By the mid-1800s in America, ladies of leisure created the lavish Baltimore album quilt. Themes reflected friendship, the family, politics and the bible, wreaths, garlands, flowers, fruit and, sometimes, public buildings, celebrations or victory scenes. Today, common methods of appliqué include cut-and-sew, inlay, shadow, stained glass or reverse (cut work), and appliqué techniques worked by both hand and machine are seen not only in traditional but contemporary styles of quilt.

Above: **Hundertwasser** *(Dijanne Cevaal, Australia). Inspiration from the world of art gives dynamic colour, pattern and design.*

Around the world Hawaiian appliqué, which originated in the early 1800s on the Kona coast of Hawaii, has continued to be a popular style. It features a bold central motif, created by a paper cut-out, which is then applied onto a contrasting background colour.

Mola is a traditional form of reverse appliqué from Central America (see picture on page 25) in which layers of solid-coloured fabrics are cut back to make patterns. These decorated panels reflect natural themes, such as stylized birds or abstract animals, as well as intricate mazes.

Similar reverse appliqué or cut work is also seen in textiles from India, China and Indonesia. In some cases, such as the Miao work from south-west China, the piecing and stitches are so small they are almost impossible to detect. Other appliqué traditions are found in Eastern Europe, North and Central Asia, where leather and felt appliqué was used to decorate robes, and animal and wall coverings.

Man's influence

Below: **New Horizons** (Sandra Meech).
A piece inspired by the Canadian landscape
artist Homer Watson.

Many of the examples in this book are
inspired by man's achievements, which
provide an unlimited wealth of
inspirational subjects to which we can all
directly relate.

Art

This enormous subject can teach us so
many things. In the past, paintings were a
visual record of a period in history, offering
a social glimpse of a time and place. The
great masters used symbolism to tell
stories, giving us not only an insight into
their world but the use of materials,
composition, colour and light across the
canvas. Contemporary artists can show us
textural paint marks or elements of graphic
design that can inspire the use of stitch or
piecing in contemporary quilts. Artists have
always been very strongly influenced by the
work of their own contemporaries. In this
spirit, you might choose to consider some
of the following suggestions:

➤ *Buy a book about the great masters
and analyse their use of design, light
and colour.*

➤ *Study and incorporate design principles
such as the 'rule of thirds' (page 126).*

➤ *Study the sculpture, both traditional
and modern, the next time you visit a
gallery – it gives a wonderful insight into
3-D installation on stitched textiles.*

➤ *Visit important exhibitions – seeing an
artist's work develop over time is of
great value. Take a notebook and
camera along with you.*

Architecture

Buildings of all ages, from ancient cathedrals to towering skyscrapers, are among man's most notable artistic achievements. Even the mud huts of tribal Africa or the Inuit igloo of Arctic Canada could become the inspiration for new work.

Above: Modern architecture in Toronto.

A recent theme of mine called 'Within 4 Walls' has given me an opportunity to address walls, considering themes of containment, protection, security and inspiration. Walls could be a home or safe haven for one person or another's prison. Consider doing all or some of the following:

➤ *Take photographs of wall details and find equivalent colours and textures in fabric – perhaps in one of the Design Classes elsewhere in this book.*

➤ *Try rubbings of stone on cloth (stabilize with freezer paper on cotton first).*

➤ *Use vinyl wallpapers to mimic texture; these can be painted with acrylic.*

Cities and urban life

City life can bring another wealth of topics, ranging from colourful markets to reflections in glass, neon lights and views from high places. Traffic or the patterns of highways can be fascinating. Power lines, metal fencing, rusty objects and tin roofs provide line, pattern and texture.

Consider that these subjects may offer layers of meaning through observation, but also comment on daily life. Look at photography books for inspiration. We can also learn a great deal about composition and the events of ordinary, everyday life through the lens of a professional photographer.

Left: **Mixed Messages** *(Sandra Meech). Torn posters, acrylic on cloth with image transfer.*
Right: **Towers of Glass** *(Sandra Meech). Photo transfer and dyed fabric.*

The media

Television commercials, billboard advertising, posters, newspapers and magazines can become a valuable resource for clever ideas, offered in a colourful, thought-provoking way. It is all about communication and, as a topic to explore on its own, contains a wealth of subject matter. Observe how graphic artists use design, colour and words to give their message impact, and study the choice of lettering, which can be beautiful on its own – it may reflect an elaborate and decorative bygone age or be clean, slick, minimal and modern. Words are frequently included in stitched textiles and can provide a chance for communication with the viewer. Graffiti – words and 'tags' in the urban landscape – reflect issues in society, and although damaging property, this colourful artistic approach is often viewed as an art form, and could stimulate us to make our own marks with greater colour and energy. Torn posters with hidden messages often suggest stitched textile themes, in which fabrics can be overlaid and overlapped.

➤ *Look more closely at the editorial layout in quality magazines and see how your eye flows across the page. Find good examples of well-designed editorial spreads and establish where the centre of interest lies, where the main headline and picture is located, and what graphics are placed in the bottom right-hand corner to make you want to turn to the next page.*

➤ *Create a torn-poster collage of sheer fabrics with written words and pictures for fun.*

Above: **Euro Poster** *(Sandra Meech). Photograph showing the layers of a torn poster. Below:* **Give Me Pink Words** *(Sandra Meech). Transfer-dyed organza and sheer layers.*

Myth and legend

Stories from the past or fables, myth and legend can become a rich topic for inspiration. Many traditional nursery rhymes are based on the politics and social history of their times. Subjects like these can inspire a series of quilts on a theme.

Hobbies and collectibles

Everyday objects around the house – kitchen tools, garden implements or pottery dishes, china or glass – could be the starting point of a new theme. Fashion and jewellery, family heirlooms (or not), decorative shoes and boots – all have a history which could influence a more in-depth theme. A still-life sketch of your household objects could reflect colour, shape or pattern for the future.

➤ Look at the room you are in at the moment and see what you find. Make notes. Describe the objects in detail – what do they mean to you? See how light from the window affects colour and shadow.

Family and health issues

Close relationships with family or friends and specific life circumstances can influence the way we view our work. Inspiration can come from celebrations – birth and marriage, anniversaries or retirement. Sometimes the death of a loved one or dealing with a health crisis can be the motivation to work. These themes are delicate and very personal but can become very strong if shared with others. Consider making a mind map (see pages 17–18) to give an objective overview of issues or concerns within the family or more general social issues that you may want to portray. Bring something of yourself into your work – personal experience sometimes needs to be worked through and there are few better ways to express your feelings than in a quilt or stitched textile.

News and politics

Emotive subjects we hear about in everyday newspaper stories concerning local or world events can be either very upsetting or uplifting. All aspects have to be put into perspective, but the use of photography and the written word is a popular technique with many quilt artists, including myself. Warning: remember copyright laws and do not copy printed information – either words and images – directly from newspapers and magazines, unless it is for personal use only (rather than for publication or sale).

Above: **Graffiti No. 1: The Warrior** *(Bente Vold Klausen, Norway). This piece is based on Nordic myth.*

Creativity plus – dynamic borders from textile inspiration

This short exercise could spark inspiration in any of the themes in this chapter. Try this on a photograph of a textile piece or a piece of patterned cloth. You will need tracing paper, a fine black pen and a template with a long and thin window (say, 2.5 x 10cm/1 x 4in).

1. Focus on a section that has movement across the length. Trace through, simplify the drawing and create a master copy.

2. With an arrow at the top, trace the shape again on a separate piece of paper, rotating the length on itself as illustrated until all four border sections are drawn. Find a detail from the original to use in the centre and trace. Copy the new 10cm (4in) design several times and have fun experimenting with coloured pencils.

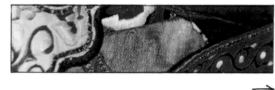

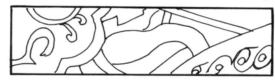

Far left: **Amauti** *(Sandra Meech).*
I see this piece as windows looking into another time and place. It is inspired by Inuit textiles.

Above: **Eco Warrior** (Pat White, Canada). This piece dramatically explores colour, line and imagery on a theme of environmental images related to the conservation of wildlife and geography. Right: **Social Statements** (Sandra Meech). Photograph of torn posters.

Above: Interpretation in coloured pencil of a painting by Alan Davie.

Design class – take one artist

Our inspiration this time will be from the world of art. First, decide upon your source of inspiration. Art from the early 1800s onward – particularly the paintings of the Impressionists and the styles that followed – included a wide range of paint techniques that can be interpreted in stitch. Contemporary graphic-design approaches might work well for those who like geometric piecing. Colour is especially dynamic in modern art, in which a mix of media reflects a wide range of subject matter.

Where to start

Don't be inhibited. For those of you who have little art experience, this isn't about drawing or copying someone's work, it is about observing how they use colour and composition for a dynamic effect. First, collect information on your own chosen theme, including writings, symbols, shapes, words and the progression of ideas already explored in a mind map. Consider emotional marks that you could make in the 'same style as…' Some obvious choices for this design class would be Miró, Kandinsky, Picasso, Braque, Monet, Matisse, Van Gogh, Klee and Hundertwasser, but you might prefer to take another favourite. Remember to buy art postcards with this exercise in mind when you next visit an art gallery.

Method

1 Studying the chosen painting, make a list of shapes, symbols or other statements on your theme and consider how you could adapt them in a similar way.
2 Look at colour and describe the artist's use of colour. Is it calm, shocking, aggressive, angry or surreal? Have complementary or analogous combinations been used? View the painting in black and white to see value and how this works. Consider making a list of the colours you would like to work with and revisit the exercise using emotive words of description.
3 Warm up first by painting some papers with resists (oil pastel) – use thicker black pens or a paintbrush to make strong marks.
4 Work freely – A3 is the best size of paper to work on, but if you prefer you can fill a letterhead-sized page with a drawing.
5 Take a window of detail from the chosen painting to abstract it further.

Left: Interpretation in coloured pencil of a painting by Vassily Kandinsky.

My example is an Arctic theme using images of igloos, caribou, and the ulu (an Inuit cutting tool) with contrasting colours of blue/turquoise for the land and orange/browns for the skins and the hunt. The representation of the two original paintings is executed in black pen and coloured pencils.

Inuit-themed pictures rendered in the style of different artists. Top: Frank Auerbach. Above: Joan Miró. Top right: Kandinsky. Right: Alan Davie.

Chapter Three
Design and Composition

What is good design? As a teacher in stitched textiles, I meet many students who are accomplished in piecing and stitch techniques, and competent in the use of colour. What they lack is confidence in design, an essential ingredient if their piece is to be a success in an exhibition. If the design doesn't work, then the viewer will walk past and move to the next quilt – no matter how well it is made.

The elements and principles of design are rules that are available to everyone. They promote good composition, helping that creative quilt or textile to become dynamic and exciting. Like everything, with regular practice, good design will become second nature.

Making collages with painted papers, textured wallpaper, newspapers and/or magazines is a great way to practise design and composition. Collages mimic fabric and give immediate colour, pattern and texture. The exercises in the design class (see page 58) are designed make you think. Using your own themes to find a personal vision will enable new work to become fresh and exciting, with focus and balance.

As with any journey, finding good design and composition is about taking one step at a time. The elements and principles of design form the first step, but looking at the way artists and sculptors use colour, composition and texture can also be an inspiration.

Above: Inspired papers – painted, resists, photocopies, commercially printed designs – anything goes.

Above: **Grand Canyon** *(Sandra Meech).*

Transfer-dyed fabric and paper collage.

The elements of design

Lines can be straight or curved, thick or thin, and they can help your eye move across the surface of your work to the focal point. Diagonal lines give movement and variety, while vertical and horizontal ones may be combined to create tension. Curved lines give a feeling of movement. Of course, to a stitched textile artist, line is often about stitch. To get started, try drawing with line on the sewing machine, stitching on plain colours with contrasting threads.

    Shape is formed by connecting lines. Shapes of different sizes can be combined in your composition: a combination of small, medium and large elements will give depth. These shapes can be geometric or organic and irregular in nature. Remember scale – larger shapes come forward; smaller ones retreat. Repeat shapes form pattern.

    In three-dimensional textiles, **form** is important and we also need to look at negative and positive shapes and the effects of light and shadow.

➤ *Consider cutting out shapes from an experimental machine-stitched piece.*

➤ *Strips and stripes, formed with a combination of painted papers and fabrics and with couched wool, could be interesting.*

➤ *Look at depth by taking three shapes of different sizes and placing them in different ways: floating, not touching in a square; touching, with the frame reduced so they flow outwards, or overlapping.*

Top: **Near North III** *(Sandra Meech). The overlaid shapes form ghostly images.*
Above: A negative image can be evocative.
Right: Paper strips laid over a black-and-white image.

Colour is a very important element of the design, and creates the mood of your piece. Study the colour wheel for different combinations in nature. Complementary colours (colours opposite each other on the wheel) or analogous combinations (three aligned colours with a touch of the one opposite) will always work well together. The subtlety of neutral colours or black and white (with small amounts of colour accent) is also popular. Sometimes, with colour, 'less is more'. With vibrant colours such as bright yellow, for example, a little goes a long way.

➤ *Have some fun at your computer with a digital photo, colour-editing for different effects. Find a hot subject and show it in cool colours. Do the opposite: for example reworking a cool seashore in warm colours.*

➤ *Move away from your own personal colour palette. Use colours that are not in your 'comfort zone'.*

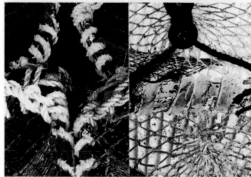

Value is about considering the effects of light, medium and dark across the surface of your work. For it to work, your piece should have these values in unequal amounts.

➤ *View a recent quilt or textile in black and white to see if you have achieved interesting values. Remember that red appears very dark in photographs.*

➤ *Work through a design from the previous chapter and make a collage with black-and-white magazine and newspaper pages.*

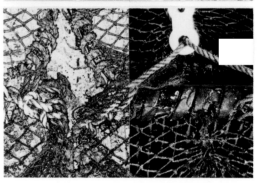

In stitched textiles, **texture** can take many forms. On a fabric surface it can be created with paint, stamp and dyeing techniques or layered combinations of mixed media, such as paper, sheers and net. Photographed textures can be transferred onto cloth (a technique I favour) or found in the many wonderful patterned commercial cottons, Balis and batiks that are available. The effects of machine quilting through high-loft wadding will also give added textural dimension (for more about texture, see chapter 5).

*Above: **Lobster Pots** (Sandra Meech). Digital effects in Photoshop Elements. Below: **Acid Rain** (detail) (Sandra Meech). Bark images manipulated in Photoshop in primary colours, transferred and stitched. See full piece on page 2.*

Above: **Standing Stones** *(Jae Maries, UK).*
The contrast of warm and cool colours with
the strategically placed stone shapes in this
piece offers a good example of design with
raw-edged fabrics and stitch.

Design principles

Good design is made up of many things, but first and foremost it suggests a creative strategy with a conscious purpose behind it. Consider the following aspects of design:

Unity and variety All good results come from a balance of ingredients that has unity and a degree of order. Some variety is necessary, however, to give greater interest. It is all about finding a balance.

Scale This is the size of the subject in relation to the space around it. For something to be a comfortable fit within its surroundings, scale is important, but shapes can be exaggerated for a more dynamic effect.

Contrast Another major factor to consider is contrast. This can attract attention by creating a 'push and pull' kind of tension between opposite elements, such as curved/straight, big/small or light/dark.

Rhythm This is also important. The intervals at which related elements occur over the surface pulls the viewer into the design to sustain interest. An accent or focal point in this rhythm will create interest. Remember that with stitch we create another agenda – a directional flow in line or repeated mark or seeding stitch.

Repetition The repetition of an element across the surface will lead the eye directly to the centre of interest. Pattern is always a major part of the contemporary quilter's palette and a design composition that includes repetition/pattern gives balance and unity to a piece.

Balance This is the way different elements in the design are distributed across the surface. Quilters who learn about traditional bed quilts will automatically consider their design in terms of the left side balancing the right side. When they begin to work in a more contemporary way, the design will be more asymmetrical and elements may need to be rearranged a few times to achieve balance. Consider the rule of thirds (see page 126) and remember that there should be a focal point or centre of interest in your work, just as there should always be a lesser point of interest in the opposite direction.

Right: **Shooting the Past** *(Claire Higgott, UK). Discharged shapes in black linen*
with thermofax prints evoke scenes from childhood once captured on film.

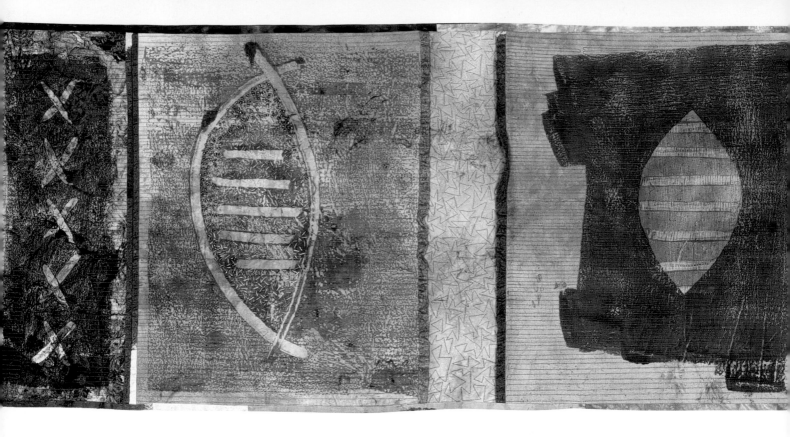

Health and safety note Brusho paints, disperse transfer dyes and Procion dyes come in powder form and should be mixed with caution. Use a mask if you suffer from respiratory problems. If you are using bleach, make sure your hands are protected and always work in a well-ventilated space. Take extra care if you are pregnant.

Surfaces for collage

This review of the different surfaces in paper and fabric that will be used in collage for design exercises will apply to both composition exercises in this chapter and all the sketchbook examples in the following chapter.

Papers that are suitable include the following types:

➤ *White or cream cartridge is smooth and therefore suitable for sketching and writing; it takes pen, pencil, paint or oil pastels and also stitches. Your paper should be thicker than copy paper, preferably 90gsm or more.*

➤ *Wall lining paper also has a smooth surface; its buff colour is warmer than cartridge. It takes paint well and is good for drawing and collage.*

➤ *Textured papers, such as wallpaper and woodchip varieties or handmade and Japanese papers, provide interesting surfaces.*

➤ *Vinyl wallpapers with texture work better with acrylic paint and, having a spongy surface, take machine stitching very well.*

➤ *Magazine and newspaper pages can be used for general collage. Full-page photos taken from travel, gardening and weekend magazines work well.*

Painting inspired papers

It is valuable to gather source material on your theme and paint an assortment of papers to dip into as you work through the design exercises. Set aside some time – many of the best ideas for new work come from inspired papers.

➤ *Choose colours that loosely reflect your theme, though some neutral pages can also be beneficial.*

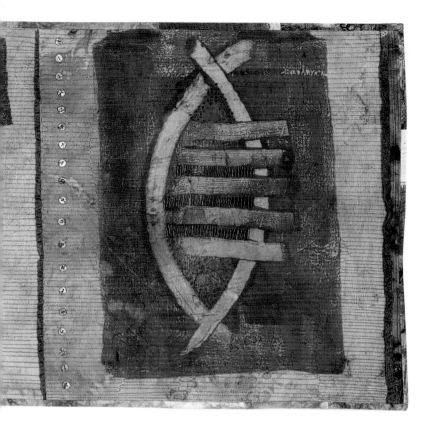

- ➤ Use resists – candle-wax before painting or oil pastels afterwards.
- ➤ Paint pages of words, both typed versions and your own handwriting.
- ➤ Paint black-and-white photocopies of images, enlarged photos or magazine references – these will be collaged.
- ➤ Newspaper pages – hidden words can be effective and could inspire a contemporary quilt or stitched textile project.
- ➤ Colour copies of your reference are also good for collage.
- ➤ Marks, symbols and shapes can be stamped, using paint (metallic paint is effective), bleach or resists (masking fluid).
- ➤ Handled with care, bleach can also be effective when applied with a pipette, string or thin acrylic paintbrush.
- ➤ Acrylic paints on paper will give a very distinctive surface.
- ➤ Acrylic on textured wallpapers can be rubbed and over-painted.
- ➤ Use stamp effects with bleach or resists (masking fluid).
- ➤ Try monoprints, which are made with thicker paints.
- ➤ Tissue paper stiffened with PVA (craft glue) can create texture that can be painted.
- ➤ Any mixed-media materials – raffia, corrugated card, fabric, net, plastics – can be added to paper pages.
- ➤ Melt wax-crayon shavings on heavier cartridge paper (use parchment to protect the iron) then add a watercolour or Brusho wash.

Right: Creative papers for collage, including black-and-white and coloured photocopies, bark cloth and transferred images.

Creating fabric surfaces for collage

Fabric can be painted as pages for stitch books or used in a mix of media with paper. Any of these combinations can be machine stitched – the possibilities are endless.

➤ *Acrylic paint can be diluted and painted onto thin white cotton – some house paints can also be used to stiffen fabric. These pages tear well when dry to give a raw edge.*

➤ *PVA (craft glue) and white paint can be mixed to stiffen fabric.*

➤ *Heavy calico (muslin), curtain linings and linens can also be painted and layered.*

➤ *Bandage muslin or scrim stiffened with PVA (craft glue) can stiffen an open-weave manipulated surface to form background pages.*

➤ *Imagery transferred onto cotton can provide an interesting page, either on its own or combined with stitches.*

➤ *LithoCoal and ChromaCoal are carbon/pastel-like materials that can be heat-fixed on cotton.*

➤ *Bonding and trapping in plastics can also give you an opaque page with fabric, net, thread and wool bits added for interest (see page 87).*

➤ *Think about over-dyeing any black-and-white or white-on-white fabrics.*

➤ *Adding sheer fabrics can give dimension and transparency to your samples.*

➤ *Transfer-dyed fabrics can offer a different texture to your collection; use cut-outs or weave shapes. You can also use the paper in the collage after the image has been transferred (see Glossary, page 126 for more information on transfer dyeing).*

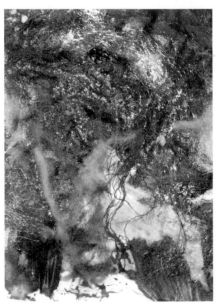

Top: A mix of batik and other fabrics, bead samples, bark cloth and transferred images.
Above: Acrylic on plastic with bonded embellishment.

Using commercial fabrics

Scraps, preferably hand-dyed pieces, Bali- or batik-style commercial cottons or fabrics with geometric patterns can inspire interesting samples. Acrylic paint on white cotton can give some very painterly results, the brush marks providing an interesting starting point for stitch. Acrylics stiffen fabric, but if the collage contains a mix of media this will make stitches more even across the surface.

Below: **Thanks to Augusta** *(Jette Clover, Netherlands). Personal memories and faded images are combined with a mixture of surfaces: rusted cloth and scrim with hand-stitch marks.*

Composition

Armed with the tools – the elements and principles of design, and a selection of collage materials at hand – we now come to the challenge of putting them together in a design. Identifying the different formats that artists regularly use in their paintings will eventually become second nature. Many of these compositions work particularly well in art quilts and stitched textiles. Recognizing them when you next visit a textile exhibition will help reinforce their use in your own creative work. Many of these composition exercises will be revisited in the next chapter.

High horizon, low horizon

Both high horizons and low horizons can be strong and dynamic. The more extreme the horizon line is, the more dramatic the composition, but as a general rule it should be around one third to two thirds in proportion. This design style evokes the feeling of a landscape, whatever the final shape of the piece.

➤ *Work two landscape compositions with different horizon positions, one with painted papers and another to include fabric and paper for stitch.*

Parallel lines or strata

Lines of different widths add variety to a composition. Straight-cut lines will have a different dynamic to that of torn paper lines. When horizontal, lines are evocative of landscape, rock strata, earth layers and nature in general; when vertical, they might be more sympathetic to architecture.

➤ *Create a long and thin landscape or cityscape with a mixture of media. Add stitching for variety.*

Above: **Low Meadow** (Elizabeth Brimelow, UK). Silk quilt, hand- and machine-stitched with appliqué and knotting. Opposite page, left: Examples of interesting compositions, including high and low horizons, parallel lines, squares, cruciform designs, S-curves, and balanced and random combinations. Middle and right: samples showing low and high horizons using a mix of media including transfer dyes, wools and painted paper.

Basic shapes

Squares, circles or other shapes can be repeated and laid one on top of the other to form a design. If shape is an integral part of your design then you will also have to think about creating a centre of interest through the choice of colour and fabric.

➤ *Think of your theme and cut out several squares in paper in different sizes; arrange them, considering the rule of thirds (see page 126) and creating a centre of interest.*

Cruciform

One of the most dynamic compositions, a cruciform shape can form the basis of any strong design. The centre of interest where the lines intersect is particularly strong. The cross shape is highly effective if viewed on a slight diagonal.

➤ *Try a cruciform composition, perhaps using analogous colours, this time in coloured papers with magazine pages and newspapers. You might also try this shape in black and white only, using newspaper and magazine headlines and type.*

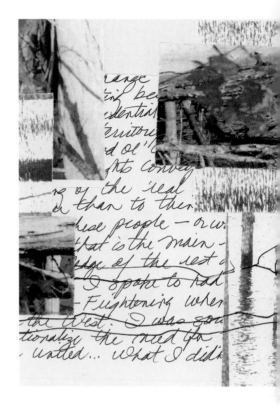

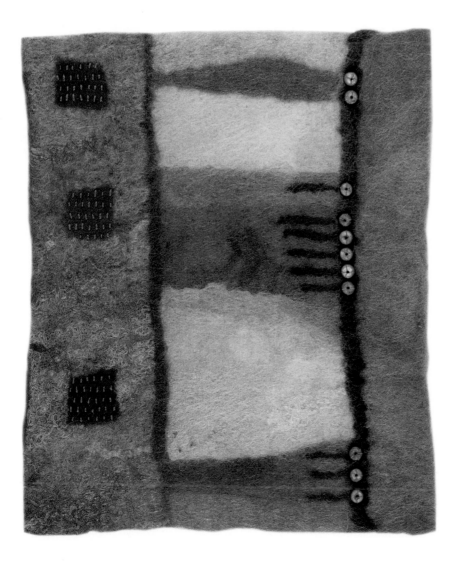

Above: A collage of reference material with a background of diary writings and line could inspire a new quilt.

Opposite page: **All Saints** *(Sandra Meech). Uplifting images for a Sunday morning. Photo transfer plus dyed and commercial fabrics with stitch.*

Left: **Synthesis #17** *(Fiona Rainford, UK). Composition in felt with stitch and embellishment.*

Above: **Sun Venezia #2** *(Fenella Davies, UK). Distressed linen sheets have been dyed and discharged to represent sun-drenched walls in Venice.*

Diagonals

Compositions with shapes, strata or the cruciform structure running diagonally across the surface can be powerful. Diagonals create tremendous movement and flow – providing you make good use of colour and pattern, the eye will move back and forth constantly.

➤ *Create a diagonal by using L-shaped apertures or a viewfinder on any designs you have already made (see page 58).*

'S' curve

Often seen in the landscape, the 'S' curve can lead the viewer into the piece and circulate the eye around all of the important detail on the surface. Artists use this for a river or a path, but abstract painters and textile artists can also use it effectively to draw us in. Used on a horizontal field, the design will resemble a landscape, but a vertical S will make the piece more abstract and less 'literal'.

➤ *Create a collage with papers in a horizontal format, then apply aperture windows to create a long and thin design. This will have more appeal.*

Central (symmetrical) motif

As quilters or embroiderers we come into these disciplines either making traditional bed quilts or decorative symmetrical patterns in stitch. These are comfortable designs, with the left and right sides mirroring each other, or a decorative ornate object with a central motif framed by more ornate pattern and decoration. All this becomes obsolete when we want to work with a more abstract modern approach.

➤ *Take a traditional motif, perhaps one from the world of textile costume, that is ordered and symmetrical in its design, and look at it through a viewfinder or L-shaped aperture. See how abstracted the original design becomes.*

Random composition

Think of the paintings of the American painter Jackson Pollock, in which the marks appear to be random. Looking closer at this cacophony of colour, you can often see small blobs of red that the eye picks up which then take you round and round. Quilt artists can use the same technique in fabric and stitch. A touch of a renegade colour in small amounts can be the detail that pulls a whole design together. The renowned British embroiderer Constance Howard would often say that a touch of turquoise, dotted in the work in small stitches, made it come alive. You may find that these little bullets of colour will often make all the difference.

Above: **Windows** *(Sandra Meech). Photo imagery painted and stitched. Below:* **Taffiti Graffiti** *(Bethan Ash, UK). Improvisation with cut and fused fabrics makes a complex but balanced surface of shapes, colour and pattern.*

Creativity plus – find the focus

Now is a good time to review focal points and centres of interest in our work. Consider the rule of thirds (see Glossary, page 126). This simple rule can provide a very dynamic starting point for design. Angle your composition or exaggerate the proportions for a more dramatic effect.

Tip How do you know when the best design has been created?

➤ *Try several different options; you will often go back to your first choice.*

➤ *Leave it for a while and view with 'fresh' eyes.*

➤ *Turn your work upside down or look at a mirror image – good design should be evident every time.*

➤ *Reduce the image through the lens of a camera – design weaknesses will become obvious. Don't forget the rule of thirds (see Glossary, page 126).*

➤ *Listen to your 'inner voice' and learn to trust your intuition to help that final decision.*

Above: Shapes of reflective buildings provide a centre of interest in this photograph. Below: two mixed-media examples of the use of the rule of thirds.

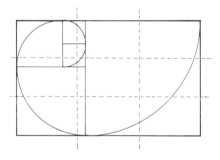

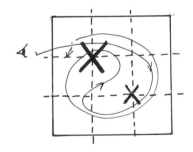

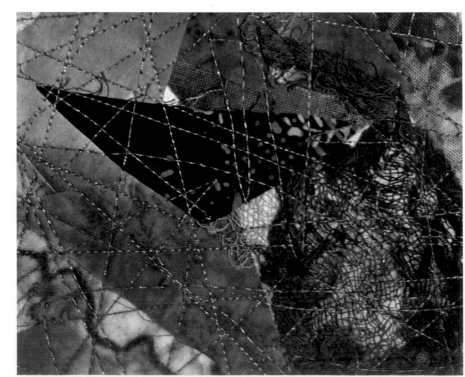

Above: **Clonrush** *(Ann Fahy). This evocative hanging piece takes its inspiration from a misty landscape by the Shannon in County Clare , Ireland. Linen was printed on a smocking machine, then hand-dyed. Opposite page, right: Randomly cut pieces of paper, disperse- and hand-dyed fabrics with scrim and wool. The composition enables the eye to flow across the surface.*

57

Design class – window to the world

The source of inspiration for this design should come from subjects influenced by man. There are so many to choose from – world textiles, modern and historic architecture, the media, posters, graffiti, ceramics, jewellery. It is best to use your own photographs. Reference materials can be obtained from many sources, but be aware of copyright issues if you want to reproduce anything that is not your own in a final textile.

For this class you may prefer to just work through exercises with coloured pencil or collage, but you may want to take some mixed media samples further and make stitch samples, perhaps between 15 and 20cm (6 and 8in) square.

The exercises illustrated are based on African textiles. You could apply the same steps to any theme as you take a section and develop it in your own creative way.

Exercise 1 Create a design

Step 1

➤ *Create your 'L's' first – suggested sizes for viewing your subject would be 2.5, 5 and 7.5cm (1, 2 and 3in) square or a long and thin aperture, 2.5 x 10cm (1 x 4in) in proportion. Consider an angled 'window' selection. See picture below.*

➤ *Find an interesting area and trace the outlines in black line. If this is difficult, use acetate and fine permanent marker pens. This will create the 'master' square reference. Do not have any diagonal lines moving into the corner.*

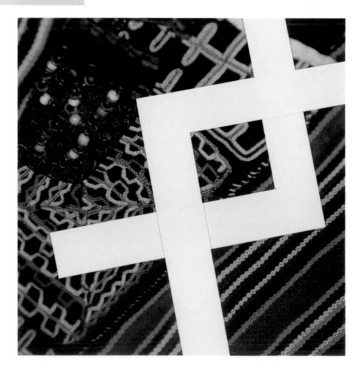

➤ *Repeat several times, finding different 'views'. The smaller the 'window' the more abstract the result.*

Step 2

➤ *Choose one of the above 'windows' in line as the master, copy it several times and enlarge to at least 15cm (6in) square.*

➤ *Use a collage of colour copies, with painted papers (magazine, textured, newspaper), or add fabric and wadding for a stitch sample.*

➤ *Consider making the design in black-and-white magazine or newspaper pages, paying attention to the value of the sections.*

Top left: A finished mixed-media sample with paper and stitch. Right top and middle: Alternative collage samples of the same design. Above: the initial drawn selection.

Above: Rusty metal from a shipyard in Cork.
Photograph by Sandra Meech. Bottom right:
templates that could inspire a series.

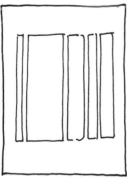

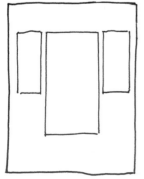

Exercise 2 Working in series

➤ *Make three templates in thin card, each about 23 x 15cm (9 x 6in), one with three long and thin sections of equal dimensions, another with different widths, and a third in a 'kimono' shape. Using photographs or colour copies of your reference materials, have some fun with different designs.*

➤ *Use tracing paper to draw sections, paying attention to a centre of interest. Take two or three black-and-white copies, keeping one for reference.*

➤ *With any of these new designs, experiment with coloured pencils, watercolour or paper collage or add fabric to provide possibilities for a future series of work.*

Although all parts of a series are designed as 'one', each individual section should stand on its own, so it's essential to pay attention to design aspects such as focal point, colour, shape and movement.

Exercise 3 Random inspiration

➤ *Gather favourite magazines together – ones with good photography and varied subjects. Geographic, traveller, homes and gardens, fashion or interiors magazines work well.*

➤ *Randomly find any page spread and choose something to use as a design source, including a section of typed headline or some of the body copy.*

Left: **The Shipping Forecast: Cromarty, Forth, Tyne, Dogger, Fisher** *(Delia Salter, UK). From a series of 32 long, thin pieces.*

Above: A selection of sketchbooks with painted pages and collage.

Right: Pencil sketch of wood and raffia.

Chapter Four
Sketch and Stitch Books

For the last few years the word 'sketchbook' has been used in many different ways. In the art world it has always been considered a personal and private document – an illustrated journal that includes ideas, jottings, words, thoughts and sketches in the form of basic small black-and-white line drawings or full-page colour illustrations. Traditionally, for ease and portability, the latter were done in watercolour. An artist in fashion or textiles might also include some fabric scraps to illustrate colour and fabric textures. It was a collection that was important purely and solely to the maker.

More recently, the term 'sketchbook' has widened to include many diverse applications, so it might be a valuable exercise to explore the various types of sketchbooks that are used today.

Diaries and journals

A diary is the most basic form of record, sometimes including a small drawing or two. It is a private place in which to document day-to-day life, including private emotions. Sometimes we need to make that connection with pen and paper to truly express our innermost feelings and ideas that could be developed further.

Journals include information that is still personal and for private viewing but they can also contain more sketches that are full of observation and detail. Colour may be included, giving the sketches more life and meaning, as well as fabric scraps for texture. They are books of collected thoughts, images and information.

The scrapbook

The 'scrapbooking' phenomenon is very popular these days, with shops dedicated solely to it. Making books to record a holiday or document family life has been a hobby for generations. Such books would include a mixture of personal memorabilia – postcards, photos, tickets, quotes, advertising or newspaper articles and found objects on a personal level. Today, scrapbook ideas can be taken further to cover less personal themes, such as ecological issues, world cultures and textiles. In fact, almost anything can become the subject of a scrapbook. Items such as grocery bills or food labels could be fun as a collage or you might make a photo montage of all the items in one room of your house, just for the record.

It is always best to create your own collection of source material for a scrapbook, despite the easy access to pre-packaged kit words and images.

Left: **Watering can and glass jar** *(Sandra Meech). A study in coloured pencil.*
Opposite page: **Near North** *(Sandra Meech). The first in a series of woodland pieces inspired by untamed landscapes in Ontario.*

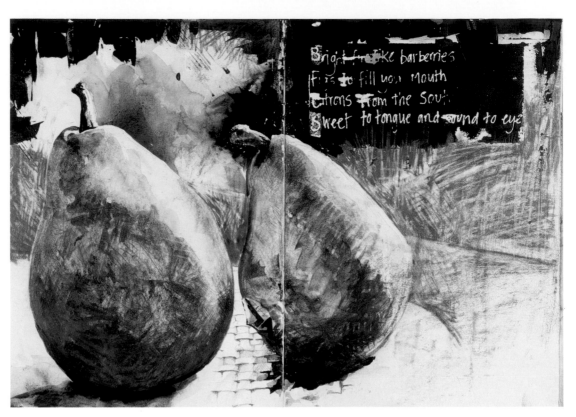

The sketchbook

This is by far the most interesting way of collecting information, a creative and inspired development from the diary, journal and scrapbook, and a way to consolidate ideas for future work.

Why are sketchbooks so important?

Once a theme is established, the sketchbook makes the perfect place to begin the creative journey – the place where personal thoughts, writings, sketches and photographs, along with newspaper or magazine articles, can be collected in a creative way. Fabric and stitch samples can be integrated with a mix of media that could eventually inspire future work. Sketchbooks provide the design potential that is essential to develop any subject further. They also provide a place in which to experiment with different materials and fabrics, and to explore stitch samples. The sketchbook can become the working design support for a single art quilt or a series of stitched textile pieces, as well as a place to include design ideas concerning the way work will be exhibited.

   Remember – wonderful sketchbooks can be achieved without formal art training, so no one need feel intimidated. With the use of collage and simple line, anyone can express themselves. Sketchbooks are personal so your sketches do not have to be professional; they are for you, and you alone, to refer to as a place for thoughts and ideas.

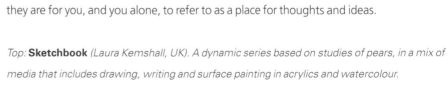

Top: **Sketchbook** *(Laura Kemshall, UK). A dynamic series based on studies of pears, in a mix of media that includes drawing, writing and surface painting in acrylics and watercolour.*
Left: These Inuit textile motifs could become stamps or stencils for sketchbook pages.

The sketchbook – uses and types

The creative sketchbook

For traditional sketchbook approaches, look to the world of art. Leonardo da Vinci's sketches, ranging from anatomical studies and portraits to technical ideas, provide an insight into his genius. In Victorian times, when ordinary people began to travel the world, other styles of sketchbooks were made, with subjects such as botanical plants or observations of textiles and costume: a sketchbook became a valuable record. Today, this personal approach to sketchbooks should not be underestimated. With approaches that include a combination of written observation, photo reference, collage and a mix of media, it is the best place in which to consolidate creative ideas.

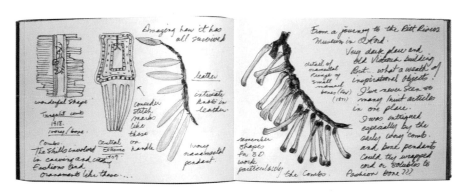

Above: A selection of sketchbooks, including spiral-bound, perfect-bound and ring-bound alternatives.
Above left: Sketchbook containing arctic studies made at the Pitt Rivers Museum, Oxford.
Left: Sketchbook containing photographs and sketches of woodlands in Ontario.

Above: **Near North sketchbook**

(Sandra Meech).

To support a finished textile piece

With many adult vocational courses based on different types of stitched textile disciplines, there has become another classification of sketchbook. These support an assessed project and are very much a working design display in book form, to be exhibited with the final work. Sketchbooks of this type are less personal, but nevertheless are experimental, artistic and impressive. They can form an elaborate book structure or a three-dimensional installation and may include hand-made or felted papers, wire, wood or other mixed-media materials. Generally, these books have great potential for inspiring future work to be developed on a theme – perhaps a whole series.

Sketchbooks as an art form

The fibre-art books that are so popular now, with many magazines and books being dedicated to their creation, are less a sketchbook than an art form in themselves. Although they may be based on a theme, rarely are any of the pages developed further into an art quilt or stitched textile piece. The pages themselves may be full of elaborate embroidery and embellishment or include the latest surface techniques, in paper, fabric and stitch, the entire collection of pages forming a bijou book. As a hobby art form, these books are lavish and exciting.

Altered books have also become an art as well – old books becoming the starting point for new approaches to paint, drawing and collage.

Above: **Creative Collage** *(Dawn Thorne, UK). A working design sketchbook.*

Above: **Feels Like Home** *(Laura Kemshall, UK). Inserted sections for dimension, fibre and stitch, inspired by the local landscape.*

Right and below: **Antarctic**
(Sandra Meech). Altered book
with collaged, painted and
textured paper and cut-out pages.

Choosing your sketchbook

There are many different forms of sketchbook, and it is up to you to decide which of those listed below is the best type for your purposes.

➤ *Perfect-bound sketchbooks are the most traditional style but, although many have a superior and heavier weight of cartridge and sketching or watercolour papers, the pages may be difficult to spread open for painting and drawing.*

➤ *The production of a hand-made book, also perfect-bound, with folded and stitched signatures, can be a very personal and satisfying accomplishment. A personal collection of papers could include white, cream and mid-tone cartridge, as well as pastel papers and thicker card. These are easier to open fully for sketching and painting.*

➤ *Spiral-bound sketchbooks, particularly those with an A5 landscape shape, are the most versatile for travel and home use. The pages are painted easily and take dimensional texture/stitches, and a book of this type is generally very flexible to use. Avoid watercolour paper, as it becomes too thick for collage and the surface is rather rough for sketching.*

➤ *A plastic ringbinder can be cut to form a flexible cover to take paper or fabric in many sizes. Mixing painted fabric with stitch pages and paper collage pages can make this into a unique sketchbook that can be added to at any time.*

➤ *Japanese stab-bound books will hold your own collection of painted and texured papers, along with fibre pages, to create an individual and unique sketchbook (see page 116).*

➤ *Folded, structured and dimensional styles of sketchbook come in many shapes and sizes, from simple accordion-fold designs to much more complicated books with overlaps and cut-outs.*

➤ *An altered sketchbook, as mentioned above, uses an old bound book as the basis for mixed media collage on a theme. Sections can be cut out and pages can be painted and folded and totally reworked.*

Remember, sketchbooks come in all shapes and sizes – the larger the pages, the longer they will take to fill. Choose a smaller one for travelling or a larger size for home use.

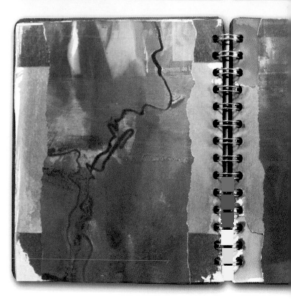

Right from top to bottom: Landscape spiral-bound sketchbook with black-and-white images coloured with pencil; colour copies on painted pages cut out for see-through effects; painted pages with oil-pastel resists.

Where to begin

Collecting references

Choosing a theme and collecting information is an important first step. This may take time, as you need to sort your photos and collect black-and-white and colour copies, including pages of your own writing, as well as articles and newspaper cuttings. Some of these will be painted, supporting the composition and collage exercises.

Painting the sketchbook

A good tip with a spiral or bound sketchbook is to paint your sketchbook pages first, choosing colours sympathetic to your theme. Inks or Brusho powder paints work well. Koh-I-Noor palettes of gem-like paints mixed with water are portable for travelling.

Top left: Memories of Rajasthan (Annette Collinge). Middle left: Kuba raffia textiles (Sandra Meech). Left: **Bark Cloth Sketchbook** *(Sandra Meech). Transferred images and fabric stitched onto a long, thin piece of bark cloth.*

Using ½in brushes, open to a spread and fill the whole page area, working quickly. Make sure you keep some spreads white, and cover others with a pale colour (for photos, writings and sketches).

To dry the pages, spread them out and suspend the book in a warm place, hanging it from the spiral coil with a long pencil or thin stick. This will take 24 hours and the dried pages will become crinkled, which adds to the character of the book.

Organizing sketchbook materials

You will require a range of pens, pencils and paints for your sketchbook.

Pencils Use HB, the softer 6B and charcoal pencils in black or white, for blending. You will also need a kneaded eraser and craft knife or sharpener.

➤ *Try varying the thickness of your pencil lines, shading for dimension and using white as a highlight on a mid-tone background.*

Pens Fine and medium black pens are very useful.

➤ *Try line exercises, making wavy, parallel or repeat patterns. You can also try adding water, using a brush to create shadow.*

Coloured pencils You should have a set of 24. Note that softer varieties will blend better.

➤ *Try making marks in colour or filling whole surfaces with colour. It is also a good idea to experiment with water-soluble (Aquarelle) coloured pencils or sticks used with a brush to create a wash.*

Chalk pastel or conté pencils Will give soft, muted effects when smudged.

Oil pastels Give strong colours, fill large areas quickly and can act as resists to paint washes.

Neocolour These water-soluble sticks work in a similar way, though they cannot be used as resists.

Candles or wax crayons work in a similar way.

➤ *Try blending or overlapping colours – scratch or scrape away in some areas for effect – and then add some paint.*

Above: Pages painted with watercolour dyes.

Above: **Wounded Caribou** *(Sandra Meech) Sketch in coloured pencil.*

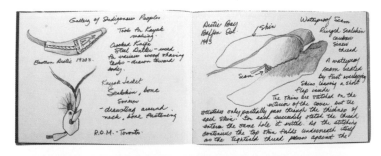

Top: *Museum sketchbook pages.*

Above: *Inuit myths and stories sketchbook.*

Take what you need

For a museum visit, take with you a small pencil case and small spiral-bound sketchbook, plus two pencils (HB and 6B) and a few coloured pencils. Take water-soluble pencils for greater flexibility. You will also require a kneaded or putty eraser, a sharpener and a small water brush if you have one.

For holiday use, take a larger sketchbook. If you can manage it, carry at least 24 coloured pencils. Also take oil pastels, three or four pencils (HB–6B), two charcoals (including white), a craft knife, a water brush, and a travel paint pallet of the Koh-I-Noor type. Newspapers, magazines and glue stick will come in handy. Also take a digital or 35mm camera to record what you see.

Wherever you go, make some simple sketches, remembering to fill the page.

Sketching, drawing and mark-making

Don't feel intimidated by the pencil – these sketches are personal and you will gain added confidence with practice. The sketches are a visual record of what you see. Different materials will give different lines or marks on the page, so experiment with a variety of materials and practise using them often. When using line, work a drawing or design right to the edge of the page.

You will find it really helpful to keep a small rectangular window template (cut one in the same proportions as your page) through which to view your subject before you choose the area to draw.

Still life

As a subject, you can choose anything from nature, a household item or a subject on your theme. Find a strong light source, such as a window, and observe the fall of light and shade.

➤ *Do one drawing in pen, using cross-hatching for shadow.*
➤ *Do another drawing using soft pencil or a carbon pencil with blended shadows. You could define edges by darkening the background tone.*
➤ *Try other media, such as gouache, watercolour or coloured pencils.*
➤ *Flatten or exaggerate perspective – look at artists such as Braque, Picasso, or Matisse and other Impressionists for ideas.*
➤ *View and draw single objects from several different angles, and then overlap them, using tracing paper.*

Right: **Lille Wall** *(Sandra Meech). Photograph manipulated in Photoshop.*

Landscape

A landscape is a great place to start as sketching outdoors can be liberating. Practise with a subject close to home, perhaps a view from your garden.

➤ *Use pages that are already painted as a starting point for a more abstract landscape.*

➤ *Use a window template to isolate an area as a starting point and use basic line marks to make simple impressions.*

Tracing paper

Using tracing paper can help you get started. Remember to use a solid line, preferably in fine pen not pencil, with a beginning and an end – not wispy half-lines. Whatever the subject matter, tracing through with simple line can be a starting point. Black and white works best – or use a light box or window for shadows.

Photo manipulation software

Reference material in high contrast, line effects or manipulated elements from photo software packages such as Photoshop Elements can provide immediate line and tone styles that can be used in collage format. This is not 'cheating': it is all part of exploring line and is an extension of drawing.

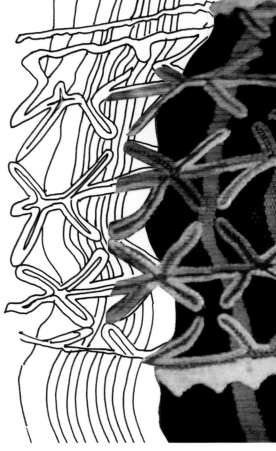

Above: African Sketchbook. Colour copy with added line. Below: Seed-pod studies in (clockwise from top left) 4B pencil, coloured pencil, pen and gouache.

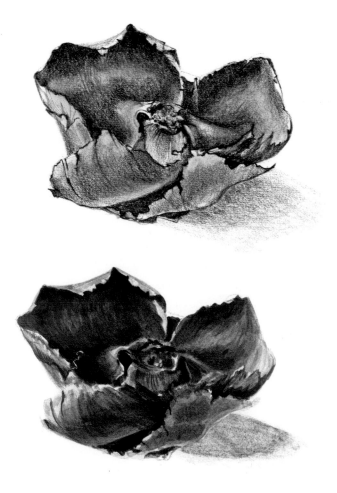

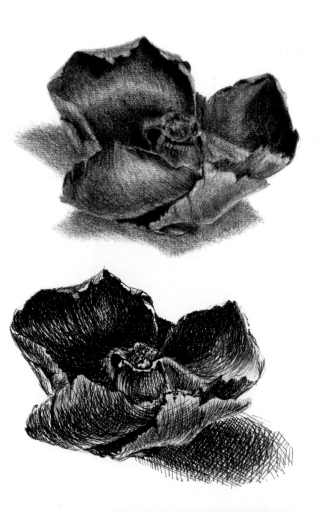

Creating stitch pages for your sketchbook

These could be incorporated into a 'sumptuous' book (see page 114). Working though composition ideas with a mix of media stitched on fabric pages can become an interesting way of working. Such pages can be part of a ring-bound sketchbook, added to a conventional sketchbook or they could fill a Japanese stab-bound book. Use composition exercises as a starting point, but incorporate a mix of media.

For the fabric pages, use prepared sheets torn to size and stiffened with PVA (craft) glue or acrylic paints. Use these as a base for stitch and collage compositions. Many forms of composition work well, including high and low horizon (see page 50), strips, diagonals, rectangular compositions, weaving, cut-away shapes, torn edges and a random selection of mixed media, stitched into place. Pierce, cut or hole-punch stiffened fabric pages for insertion in a binder or stab-bound book (see page 116).

For information on painted papers and enhanced fabrics, see pages 46–49.

Creativity plus – a page a day

Above: Mixed media stitch pages in a plastic binder.

Try filling an A5 or smaller page every day for a month – your progress will surprise you. Try making a stab-bound sketchbook (see page 116–117): some pages could be of paper, others might be fabric pages with mixed media and stitch. These could be worked separately and bound together to make a memory book of that period of time.

I have included a series of mixed-media collage stitch samples opposite – each of which took about 40 minutes – based on a theme of the Arctic and global warming. You can see how much freer they become as I get 'warmed up'.

Left: **Inspired sketchbook** (Laura Kemshall, UK). Above: **Kilmartin sketchbook**
(Sandra Meech). Ancient cup-and-ring symbols in stone. Below: **Arctic pages**
(Sandra Meech). Sketchbook pages decorated with collage and stitch.

Design class – an inspired sketchbook

A problem frequently arises when you have all your inspiration, collected writings and reference, black-and-white and colour copies, and painted pages ready: where to start? If you are at a loss, working through collage and composition exercises with some extra simple drawing and writing is a good first step. A mind map will also refresh your memory.

Collage and composition

Working through a selection of paper collage exercises will trigger ideas for a future piece of work. Contemporary quilts come in many shapes and sizes. They are exhibited in series, and sometimes have cut-out and see-through areas. Sketchbooks are a great place in which to explore this potential in paper and collage. Before you start, create a window template that is the exact size of the sketchbook page. With the card that is left over, make several other windows in the same proportion (see illustration).

Points to remember

➤ *Although shown as landscape-shaped page spreads, all exercises can be adapted to square or portrait-shaped pages.*

➤ *Include a word or two on each spread to remind yourself (certainly in your first sketchbook) which composition exercise you are practising.*

➤ *Jot down notes on the page, including any comments on planning, future piecing or stitch ideas.*

➤ *The rule of thirds (see page 126) as a design focus.*

1) Weaving

This is a simple first step and the only exercise listed here to be inserted into your sketchbook after you have finished.

➤ *Tear sections of three painted papers on your theme into strips of differing widths, tearing one page vertically and the others horizontally.*

➤ *Take an letterhead-sized piece of paper as the background, and add glue to the top.*

➤ *Select the thick and thin vertical pieces and weave down the page with the remainder.*

➤ *Paste the whole collage/weaving onto the background.*

➤ *Using the window template, find an interesting section – perhaps on an angle – and cut it out.*

➤ *Any extra pieces can be added to the second page.*

➤ *Use the second page to extend line and draw into the background, reflecting your theme.*

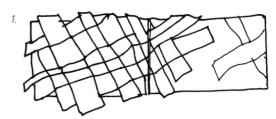

2) Blocks of reference

This exercise in composition lets you take away and add sections, then fill in the spaces with simple line drawings.

➤ *Taking an section of your reference (a colour copy or magazine page), cut out squares and rectangles from the surface, being careful not to cut through the entire piece.*

➤ *Paste the skeleton page on one side of the spread, with the remaining squares on the other.*

➤ *Extend the lines with a fine pen, using the reference back and forth.*

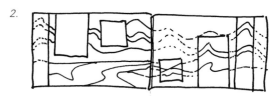

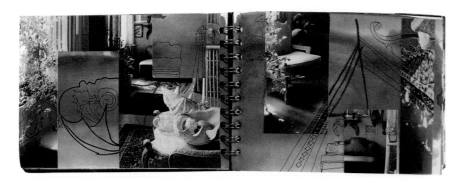

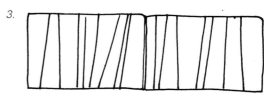

3) Vertical/parallel lines

➤ *Torn sections of paper reference (vary the widths) can be added to a painted background. Use writings, photos, patterned paper or textured paper if you choose.*

➤ *Some drawing could be added for effect.*

➤ *Use a larger image in some parts of the double-page spread.*

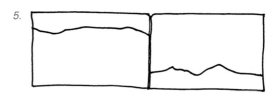

4) 'S' curve diagonal

➤ *Lay three prepared papers on top of each other. Cut with a craft knife or scissors through all layers. You could cut ordered curves or let pieces fall more randomly. Lay the shapes on a dark or coloured background to observe negative spaces.*

➤ *Assemble a mixture of colours and surfaces together for interest. You may want to extend some elements with line marks in pen or oil pastel.*

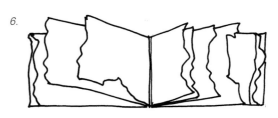

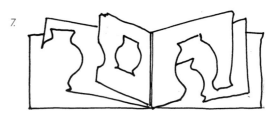

4.

5.

6.

7.

5) High horizon and low horizon

➤ *You may want to do a simple high-horizon collage by laying leftover scraps on a colourful page.*

6) Torn pages in series

➤ *Several pages in sequence could be torn into different widths, the torn edges adding interest.*

7) Cutting away

➤ *Shapes could be cut out of some pages and pasted on others. This could inspire a layered quilt.*

8) Tracing and drawing

➤ *Trace the same shapes several times and layer them for a more abstract design. Extend with a black-and-white photocopy, coloured or painted.*

9) Enlarged detail

➤ *Use a window template to isolate an area that could be enlarged. Scale it up in sections. Perhaps a square could be rotated on itself for an inventive block design.*

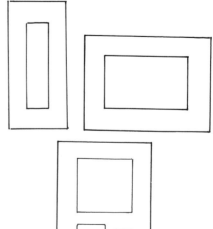

Right: **Amauti** *(Sandra Meech).*

8 and 9.

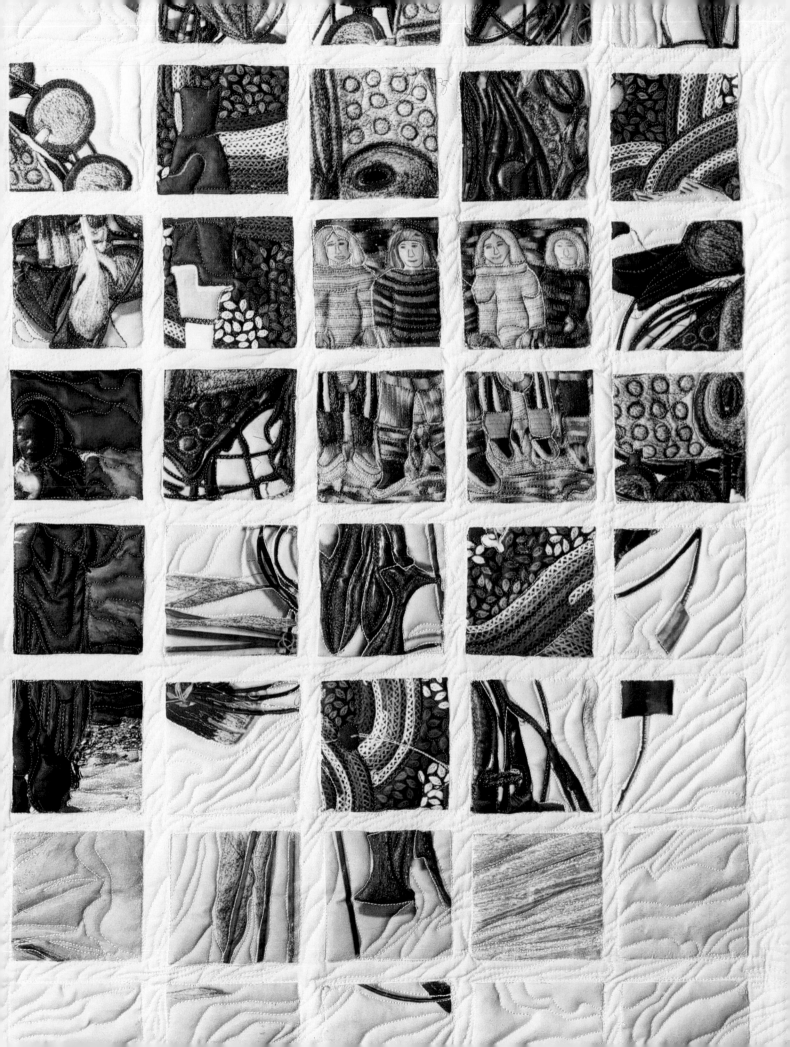

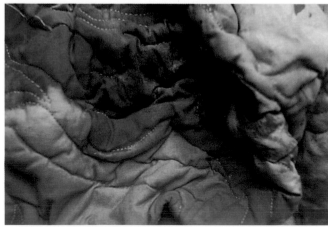

Chapter Five
Texture and Dimension

Texture and dimension go hand in hand. Texture is part of the actual surface and, when it is raised, gives a sense of dimension that lends a creative edge to contemporary art quilts. Traditionally, there were many ways to raise the surface of a fabric. These include Japanese folded methods, Suffolk puffs (also known as yo-yos) and cathedral window, as well as many other manipulated fabric techniques. Victorian 'crazy' piecing incorporated a variety of different fabrics – velvets, silks and sateen – with embroidery embellishment. Baltimore quilts sometimes included raised and applied motifs with dimensional embroidery stitchery. Both hand and machine quilting can add texture and pattern to the surface. Contemporary two-dimensional wall-hangings (worked with a depth of up to 5 or 7.5cm/2 or 3in) or three-dimensional installations sometimes include mixed media – paper, plastics or metal. In the traditional world of embroidery, heavy embroidery stitch techniques, such as crewel work, smocking, ruching and beading, and the use of braid, knots and other surface embellishment have always been popular. Many of these disciplines are now finding their way into modern quilt art.

Above: Linen and silk, pleated and dyed (Ann Fahy, Ireland).
Left: **Gatherings** *(Sandra Meech) Painted fabric stitched through Wireform.*
Right: **Orange Fizz** *(Sandra Meech). Mixed-media dimension, acrylic paint, Tyvek and scrim.*

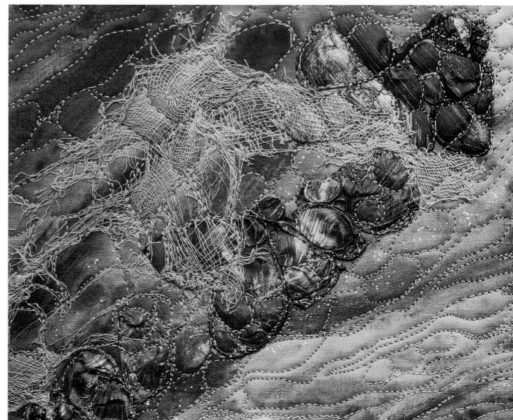

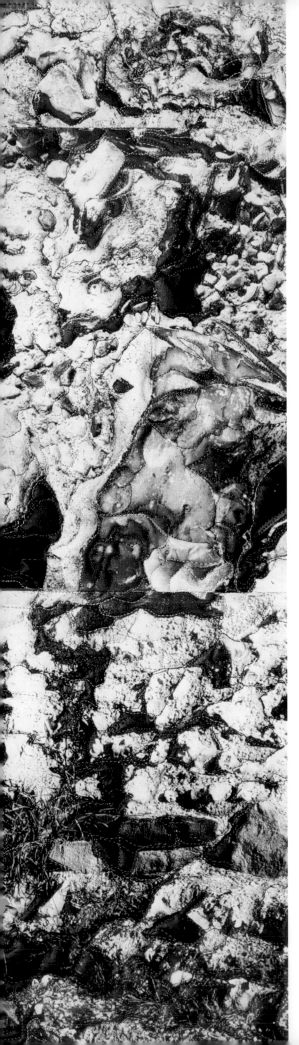

Why do we use texture?

Light and shade

The surface of bed quilts and wall hangings catches the light in different ways. Natural light from the window or overhead spotlights at an exhibition will give dimension to work, whether stitched by hand or machine. Methods of photo-transfer that plasticize cotton will also attract light, especially if a high-loft wadding is used. The general use of plastics for trapping things, using beads, sequins and metal on the surface, or traditional stitch motifs that include shisha mirror glass (popular in Eastern textiles) is another way to raise the surface. (Photo-transfer techniques and working with plastics are explained in the glossary on page 126.)

➤ *Consider painting a small piece of fabric with some pearlized or iridescent paints; machine quilt through a sample that includes a thicker wadding to see how light enhances the surface.*

➤ *Try combining a selection of different fabrics in a small sample and see how light affects velvet, chintz, linen weaves, silk, glazed cottons and lace.*

Highlight a detail

Traditional embroidery motifs using thicker wools and stranded threads make a strong visual statement, the thick threads being raised from the background. An appliquéd motif that has been gently stuffed also creates dimension, as seen in Baltimore quilts.

Copying texture

Mimicking specific detail in a personal subject – the bark of a tree, pebbles on a beach, rock strata or rusty walls – can be an interesting challenge. There are several ways of creating texture. These include using a mix of media, for example texture gels, painted textured papers, fabrics such as lace, net and scrim (muslin) and PVA (craft) glue. For a very firm backing, heavy interfacing fibres already possess structure and can be painted, transfer-dyed and stitched; they work well for installation pieces. Extra trapunto stuffing could also be used after stitching to add interest. Another way to achieve texture could be with Wireform. Used as an extra quilt layer, it is stitched and the surface is then manipulated (see page 96). Important considerations include the size and weight of the piece, and how easy it will be to transport.

➤ *Consider using a patterned commercial fabric and adding texture – pebbles, grasses and brickwork in black-and-white and colour – created with extra fabric paints. Watered-down artist's acrylics or pearlized and iridescent fabric paints work well.*

Left: **Roman Wall: Containment** *(Sandra Meech). Photo transfer with painted and dyed fabrics, from the Within 4 Walls series.*

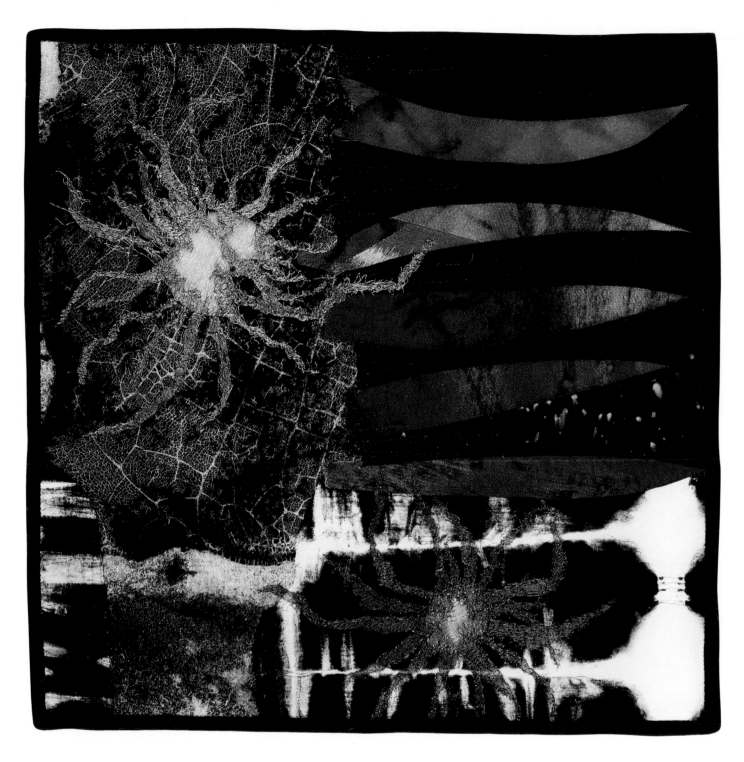

Looking through layers

There are two ways that you might be able to 'see through' an art quilt. The first is to use sheers, net and voiles to give a transparent quality, even when the fabrics are pieced or applied in a conventional way. Another way to be able to look through a hanging is to have sections cut out. This is usually done after the quilting is finished. This technique is particularly effective when the shadow cast on the wall becomes part of the design.

Begin by experimenting in a sketch or stitch book. Look for remnants of sheer fabrics or lace with which to begin. These could be painted or, if the fabrics include polyester, transfer-dyed for interest (see Glossary for more on transfer dyeing).

Above: **Rage and Outrage #2** *(Linda Colsh, Belgium). A small section is cut out and sheers have been added.*

➤ Have a sense of fun – pockets, perhaps folded or pleated, containing hidden treasures or random raw-edged pieces, can add interest. Another technique is to cut up bits of fabric (net, sheers, scrims) and paper and let them fall where they may onto iron-on interfacing. Iron flat, using parchment to protect the iron.

The illusion of texture can also be an interesting addition. An image from a personal theme transferred onto cloth creates a very exciting form of texture. Photoshop Elements or Paint Shop Pro can provide wonderful filters and effects to use that include embossing, outline and shadow impressions. These can provide a good starting point for ideas.

➤ Try taking a photograph of a textile that has texture, transfer it onto cloth and add even more texture and stitch.

Left: **Bruges Brick: Security** *(Sandra Meech).*
From the Within 4 Walls series.
Below: **Drying Rack** *(Sandra Meech). Image transfer stitched through Wireform.*

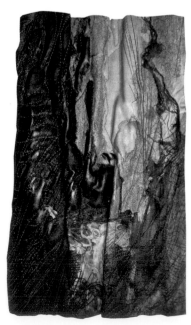

When to use texture?

It is important to ask yourself what type of dimension is needed to impact the subject in a particular way. Many smaller stitched-textile pieces have many textural techniques added so indiscriminately that the work is cluttered and confusing. Embellishment should be used with discretion and should inform the theme and integrity of the work. Dimensional surfaces should have a purpose for being and also support the design and colour choices. Texture should not be seen as an added extra. Often, 'less is more'.

For a large contemporary quilt, it could be technically difficult to use a great deal of texture over a large area – not only hard to sew by hand or machine, but also to transport to exhibitions. Smaller works allow for a wider choice of methods and materials. Given the huge range of texturing materials now on the market, it takes an experienced and discerning eye to select the most appropriate ones.

Texturing materials

It is easy to be seduced by the many materials and techniques on the market. In the world of contemporary embroidery, we seem to be spoilt for choice. Materials that are appropriate to contemporary quilting have to be carefully selected because of the size of quilt art wall hangings and the flexibility required. Nevertheless, it may be possible to incorporate different methods when the pieces are smaller, and this may provide a needed diversion. Remind yourself what is appropriate to your theme and don't be tempted to add texturing materials just for the sake of it.

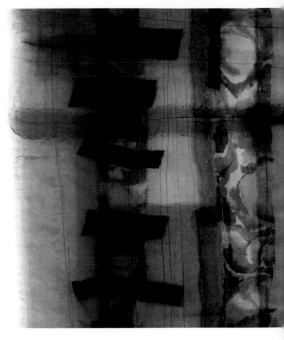

Above: **Swimming** *(Esther Silverton, UK). Fabric trapped in sheers, expressing light, movement and distortion in a swimming pool.*

1.   *2.*

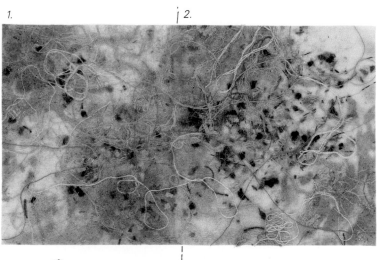

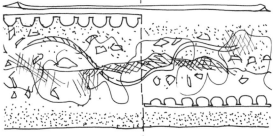

Left: This piece of work, divided into two halves, shows different techniques for trapping and bonding to create texture. The left-hand half (1) shows trapping, which gives a stable surface. The layers, from top to bottom, are parchment; bubble wrap (bubbles down); bonding powder; a mix of wool, thread and Angelina fibres; more bonding powder; a background of dyed fabric. The right-hand half (2) shows bonding, which gives a more unstable surface. The layers, from top to bottom, are parchment; bonding powder, a mix of wool, thread and Angelina fibres; more bonding powder, bubble wrap (bubbles up); bonding powder; a background of dyed fabric. Both surfaces were covered with parchment and ironed with a firm, hot iron to allow the fabric elements to meld with the plastic for an embellished effect.

Listed below are a number of materials on the market that can add dimension to both paper and fabric. Some might be more appropriate at the collage and paper design stage, with others in a finished stitched piece. Be aware that these may create a hardened surface, preventing easy machine quilting.

Texture media These can be applied by brush to give a raised surface. Sand, gravel and glass effects are more appropriate for a mixed-media piece or a small stitched textile.

Acrylic paint and gesso These may also raise the surface but are difficult to stitch through unless used thinly.

Puff paint This binder can be painted onto fabric and expands when heated with a heat gun. Some interesting effects can be achieved on a very small scale.

Paper etch This gel dissolves a design on paper, giving dimension.

Tyvek This fibrous paper prevents condensation and is used in the building industry as well as in envelopes to protect legal documents (see page 95).

Plastics These will also give a form of raised dimensional surface to cloth. You could use bonding powder to bond materials such as bits of sheer fabric, net, wool or thread to the surface of bubble wrap (use parchment to protect the iron) or sandwich bits between fabric and plastic (trapping). Samples of both techniques could be pieced into a contemporary quilt, but only the latter would form a stable and relatively practical surface.

Lacy and lattice fibres These can be created in a number of ways and added to the surface of a quilt.

➤ *Scrim or bandage muslin stiffened with PVA (craft glue) and manipulated can be added to the surface to create interesting lattice effects.*

➤ *Thread lace is created with cold-water-soluble film and can be easily made with free-motion embroidery methods (see illustration).*

Knitting Knitting created with interesting wools, string or fine metal wires can lend additional texture, especially with the addition of embellished bits and pieces.

Dimensional stitches Stiches such as French knots add texture to a surface. Couching a mix of wools, threads or even paper could also add interest. Macramé knotting with a variety of materials could also be considered. When a stitch is heavily worked, the resulting light and shade creates new dimensions. It is also worth experimenting with rolled paper and thicker wools.

Left: **Cup and Ring: Kilmartin** *(Sandra Meech). Photo imagery, scrim and wool. Right:* **Cruciform: Security** *(Sandra Meech). From the* Within 4 Walls *series, this piece shows the Cruciform Building, a former teaching hospital and now part of University College London. The plasticized surface creates texture when stitched.*

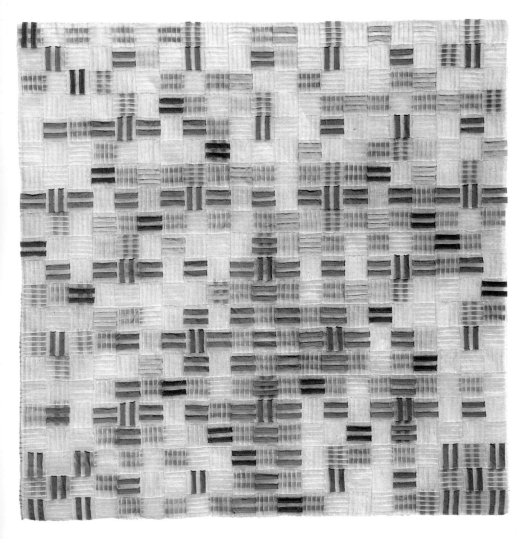

Free and abandoned techniques

These could include many possibilities such as beads, fabric, buttons or ribbon. Use scraps of felt or hand-made paper to give pattern and texture. Look at the world of contemporary embroidery for alternative embellishments.

Overall texture Pieces of fabric, lace, scrim and net can be couched and stitched to a surface. These are more appropriate for small works. By overlapping simple stitches – perhaps cross stitch, fly stitch or chain stitch – textural interest can be achieved.

Cord, tassels, jewellery, braids and shells Use these to add texture to a piece – look to world textiles for inspiration.

Dye effects Batik, tie-dye and marbling methods of dyeing can create the illusion of depth.

Above: **Nine-Patch Variation** *(Inge Hueber, Germany). Dyed cotton and organza.*

Below: **Elvis Has Left the Building** *(Kate Cox, USA). Detail of embellished jacket.*

Metal Metals, particularly softer varieties such as copper, brass and silver, are available in fine sheets called 'shim' (0.05mm works well for machine stitching) or as thin wires. Experiment first to see if the effects would work on a larger art quilt. Techniques for embossing, burning and cutting metals could be explored (new implements, cutters and embossing tools may be required).

Manipulating surfaces

There are many ways of manipulating the surface to give dimension in contemporary quilting. Traditional methods, including Kantha stitching, have become popular in contemporary art quilts. As well the mark-making darning stitches, seeding stitches can be seen now in many creative pieces (see page 103 for more about Kantha stitching).

PVA-stiffened fabrics

Most natural fabrics respond well to being stiffened with PVA (craft) glue. When dry, the fabric will need to be couched or basted into position on the surface and can never be ironed. It will be difficult to machine into and may be of limited use in large pieces, but it is sometimes worth a try.

➤ *Try stiffening dyed fabrics. Once dry, the resulting surfaces can be enhanced with additional paint including metallics.*

Folded patchwork

There are many different methods of folding fabric. Think of a theme and find one or two that might reflect your subject. Flowers have often been depicted in many Japanese folded styles and create interest in two-dimensional pieces. It might be worth trying to adapt folded patchwork to depict architecture and buildings.

Right: **Slate Modern** *(Sandra Meech). Rock and slate imagery on cotton with transparent squares, used as a room divider.*

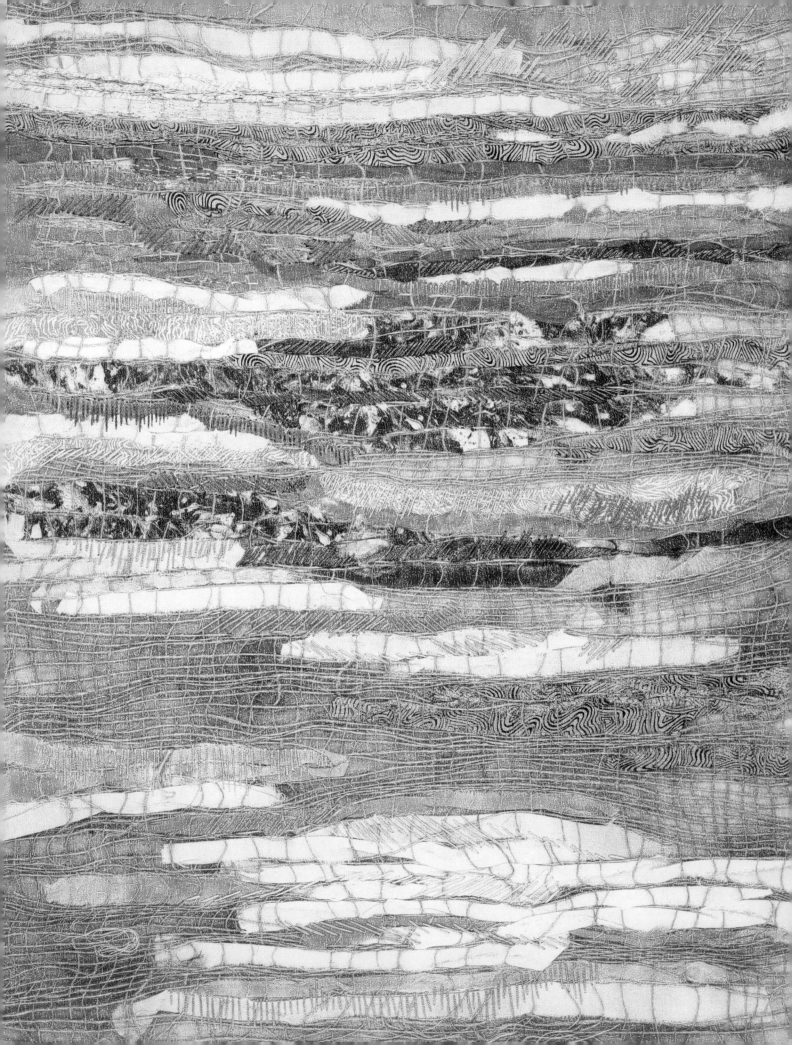

Pleats and tucks

Often thought of as belonging to the same family as folded patchwork, pleating can benefit fabric surfaces in clever ways. Remember that pleated and tucked areas will catch the direction of light and can be transformed accordingly.

Wireform

A layer of wire mesh can be trapped inside the quilt sandwich (under the wadding) to provide a surface that can be quilted as usual and then manipulated in extreme ways. The width of the opening is limited by the nature of the sewing machine, so often the widest area that can contain wire mesh is about 45cm (18in).

Stitching and shrinking

Today, art quilts take all shapes and sizes, including three-dimensional pieces that come out from the wall and those created as installations that people can walk around. Techniques can bring together some extraordinary methods of stitching with fabrics that may have been dyed and shrunk to create texture.

Layering

Many forms of appliqué can be used to give dimension to a surface. A colour or patterned section, applied to a dull or solid background, will give the illusion of dimension, becoming a valuable design tool. Contemporary shapes, such as crosses (or 'band-aids', as I call them), can link two sections and bring a stronger design flow.

Left: **Tundra Springtime** *(Sandra Meech). Strips of cotton woven through hessian with sheers and stitch.*
Right: **Convolutions 9: Pathways** *(C June Barnes, UK). Explorations into texture through shrinkage and manipulation.*

Creativity plus – Tyvek with integrity

Often, the presence of these texture-enhancing materials is criticized because they are included indiscriminately and it is obvious that they have been added without consideration being given to the background. They may look as if they are just there for a clever effect, when they should be included only when they are blended and worked into the background with colour and stitch.

Paint a sample of white cotton 20cm (8in) square, and a piece of Tyvek 10cm (4in) square at the same time with acrylic paint – the two surfaces will have a sense of unity.

Heating Tyvek

If you want convex (bubbles up) shapes, then heat Tyvek with its good side down, after cutting into the sides. Concave shapes (craters) happen when you heat with the painted side upwards. Making sure the Tyvek is thoroughly dry, place it between two pieces of parchment and heat with a hot iron, just hovering over the surface. You can achieve similar results with a heat gun. The Tyvek will soon start to distort, providing it doesn't stick to the parchment. Take special care with heat guns, and work in a well-ventilated room.

Adding stitches

➤ *Create a fabric sandwich with a high-loft wadding and pin Tyvek into position – perhaps with three sections of Tyvek on painted cotton.*
➤ *When stitching (by machine only), the needles will break if you stitch into any of the very hard plastic parts.*
➤ *Repeat the circular shape of the distorted Tyvek and use a thread that blends with both surfaces.*
➤ *Some hand stitches – French knots, beads or seeding stitch – could be added.*

Left: **Melting Away** *(Sandra Meech). Paint, scrim and Tyvek. Below: Tyvek and background cotton both painted with acrylic at the same time, allowing textures to integrate after stitching.*
Right: **Hot Blue** *(Sandra Meech). Painted surfaces merge together when stitched.*

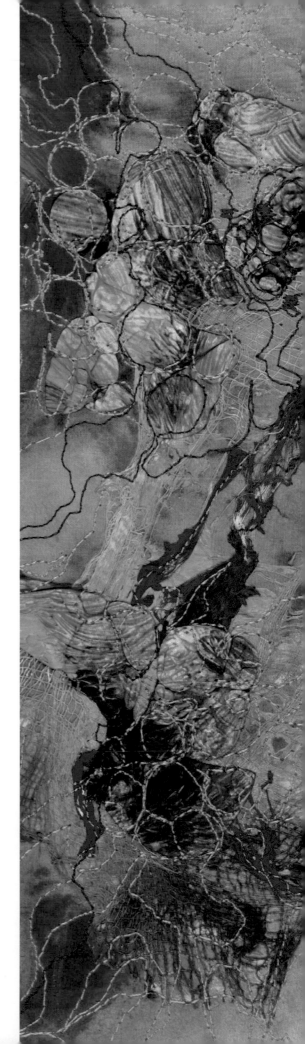

Materials

- A suitable 20 x 25cm (8 x 10in) surface. This might be acrylic-painted cotton, with oil pastel (heated and fixed) marks for interest, or a mixed-media composition, including bonded and trapped plastics, and painted or transfer-dyed fabrics, with paper on a theme, or a transferred image, such as a photograph with writings transferred to fabrics
- Wireform, 6mm (¼in) smaller all the way around than the surface piece. There are many varieties to choose from and the finer mesh type made from aluminium or copper works well. (Other types may not be as appropriate for layering and machine quilting)
- High-loft wadding, cut to size
- Backing fabric – a firm cotton, cut to required size

Below: **Wired Bowl** *(Sandra Meech). Painted fabric layered with Wireform then manipulated.*

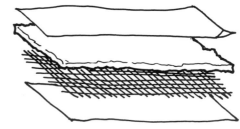

Design class – off the wall with Wireform

This workshop will explore in simple ways the use of Wireform in a 20 x 25cm (8 x 10in) stitched textile piece. This could provide an opportunity to use a collage or mixed-media composition prepared in an earlier experiment as a surface to manipulate.

Method

1 Layer and pin the four pieces together, with the backing fabric on the bottom, then the wire mesh, followed by wadding and with surface composition on top (see diagram, bottom right).

2 Use simple machine threads, such as Gütermann, Madeira tanne or embroidery threads with a 70–80 needle. Avoid twisted threads, metallics, or rayon threads.

3 Machine stitch diagonally across the surface, picking up some detail along the way. Remember that the sample will be manipulated later, so any fancy stitching may not be at all obvious.

4 Stitch to the edges. When you have finished, trim the whole piece slightly (the Wireform is slightly smaller, so this should not affect cutting). You may want to finish off the edges with a tight or open zigzag stitch.

5 Manipulate the finished piece, perhaps bringing the size closer to a more extreme 20cm (8in) square shape.

These small pieces can look very effective when mounted on a larger simple piece of wood or into a box frame, away from the background (use foam core board to raise the shape from the background). You could also try the following ideas:

- *Make a long and thin composition, including the mesh only in some places, stitched and wall-hung with wood, or plastics. Remember that hand stitching can be added for extra texture.*
- *To make an embellished bowl, work with a circular piece of Wireform (perhaps 20cm/8in in diameter) and a much larger surface fabric composition, say a circle 30cm (12in) in diameter. The reverse fabric should be something interesting, such as a batik, a dyed fabric or shot silk. The edges could have irregular shapes. Stitch the layers together as above, finishing with a zigzag stitch. Manipulate the finished piece, moulding it over a small basin to create the bowl shape. Further stitches and beads could be added for effect.*

Right: **Rust Cork Shipyard**
(Sandra Meech). Photo
transfer with layers of fabric,
stitched through wire and
manipulated to cast
shadows.

Above: **Extravagance** *(Kate Cox, USA). Rich, luscious colours and textured wools are loosely knitted together with added fabric embellishment.*

Left: **Thanks to Augusta (detail)** *(Jette Clover, the Netherlands). Imagery and raw-edged fabrics overlaid with writing and big stitches.*

Right: **Noughts and Crosses** *(Sandra Meech). Paper, fabric and stitch composition.*

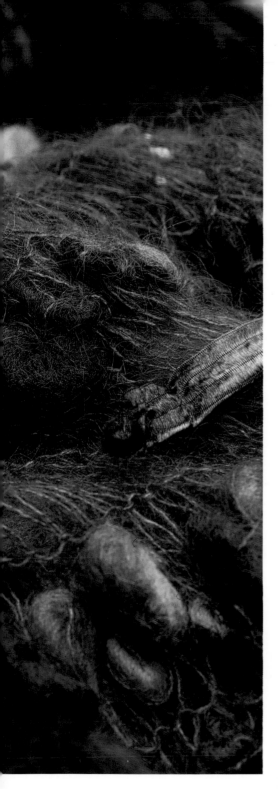

Chapter Six
Exploring Stitch

The final stitch choices that we make can be the determining factor which turns that very good art quilt into one that has ticked all the boxes, pulled out all the stops and gone that one step further than anything you have done before. Being creative and adventurous and meeting new challenges 'head on' can be highly satisfying, especially as we can experiment with so many new techniques in smaller pieces. This is the time to try something new in stitch and see where it takes you.

Earlier mark-making exercises and mixed-media collage with tracings and line can start the ideas flowing, but actual 'play' with hand and machine embroidery stitches will be the next step.

There are so many exhibitions to visit, contemporary embroidery books to read and art quilts in abundance, that it can be overwhelming. Continue to think about your theme, the choices you have made with design and colour, the materials you have selected, and the overall structure and dimension of your final work. With these in mind, the appropriate hand or machine quilting stitches will be easier to determine.

Hint: it is always easier to set some materials or collage scraps aside throughout all the stages to use when practising stitch samples.

Exploring traditional hand-stitch techniques

All the stitches that we use and enjoy today in quilting or embroidery have their origins in traditional world textiles. Traditional embroidery stitch techniques have greatly influenced contemporary quilting and stitch textiles, and this chapter won't cover them all. Only the more popular stitches and piecing styles have been selected – ones that have been skilfully adapted to meet the demands of quilt and fibre art. Reviewing some of these techniques, their historical origins and how they are used today will illustrate the creative possibilities when you explore stitches for your own work.

Left: **Harvest** *(Annette Collinge, UK).*
Inspired by a field in the countryside, this quilt is made up of applied blocks and an inspired collection of hand embroidery stitches.
Below: **Reflections** *(Kit Vincent, Canada).*
Paint on cotton with big-stitch hand quilting.

Running stitch This is perhaps the earliest documented stitch and is evident in many cultures. There are many varieties of this simple stitch, which passes in and out of two or more layers of fabric, giving the appearance of a mark or broken line.

Back stitch This gives a strong line mark, and can bring additional dimension and highlight details, shapes or colours on the surface.

Kantha stitch This is seen in textiles from Bangladesh and Eastern India, where it also became a decorative feature used to depict nature or tell stories, with the addition of variations such as back stitch to give detail on the surface. Traditionally, the kantha stitch was also meant to represent water – a life force that ripples in the light. Today, this simple darning stitch is effectively used in contemporary wall hangings, providing dimensional manipulated 3-D surfaces, in finer wall-hung textiles or as a simple stitch worked through sheers and delicate fabrics.

Sashiko This Japanese running stitch, taken through layers of fabric, has very early origins. To create warm, practical clothing, two layers of deep blue indigo-dyed cotton would be stitched together with a contrasting white thread. Stylized patterns of fans or hemp leaves remain popular today.

Quilting stitches These were originally used to hold together two or three layers of material, traditionally a top fabric, a middle layer, which was often wool fleece or a blanket and provided warmth, and a backing fabric. The piecing of scraps of recycled clothing, sewn together with a short darning stitch and often arranged in block patterns, created the top layer of a bed quilt.

Seeding is a series of delicate or bold marks used as shading, to fill in colour, or to give a directional emphasis, creating a sense of movement across the surface. Sometimes, a simple darning stitch is used in a more abstract way, moving in and out of the design and giving the impression of an image in a background or a line that trails in and out.

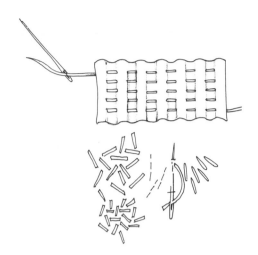

Top: Darning, the basis of all quilting stitches, including those seen in Indian kanthas.

Above: Seeding stitch provides a mark as well as integrating colour and texture.

Left: **Walberswick Furrows (detail)** *(Elizabeth Brimelow, UK). Cut-out shapes applied with hand and machine stitch. Right:* **Time and Tide** *(Sandra Meech) This piece includes familiar sashiko motifs.*

Left: **Sunlight and Shadow cushion** *(Julia Caprara, UK). Dramatic colour combinations with textural embroidery stitch make this a wonderful dimensional piece.*

Below: **Memories (detail)** *(Janet Atherton, UK). Hand stitch on calico.*

Embroidery stitches

There is a huge number of stitches to choose from, but their use in contemporary quilting will be relative to the scale and size of the final piece of work. The larger the quilt, the larger the stitch: small delicate stitches may not be effective except in small wall-hung stitched textile pieces. Here, decorative embroidery stitches can either be used to fill areas, with shiny threads massed and overlapped to catch the light, or as an outline for shapes, often combined with beads or couched materials for added dimension and interest.

➤ *Consider working a series of the same embroidery stitch with different thicknesses, colours and twists of threads. We are spoilt for choice with luscious threads and you will find that the results will be very different, according to the thread used.*

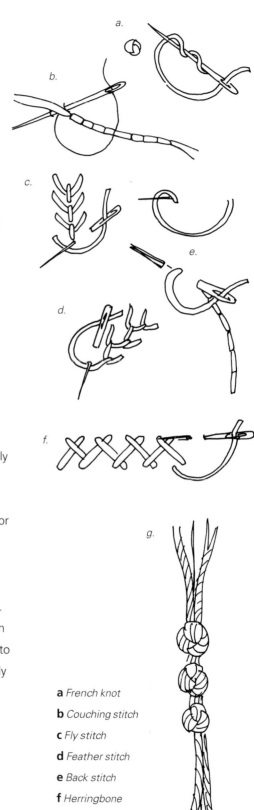

Chain, herringbone or blanket stitch These can make a particular mark or be overlapped to create dense areas of stitching. They are often used to link applied pieces together or attach them or they can act as a decoration on their own.

French knots These can also give dimension on the surface and may be very effective when combined with couched materials or Tyvek dimension effects, easing the transition from texture to a background. The stitches might be better added after machine quilting. Used in conjunction with couched materials and simple darning-stitch marks, the use of French knots in small contemporary stitched textiles can certainly be explored.

Couching Couching stitches can be used to add a mix of materials to the surface, giving the extra texture needed. Knotted or textured wools can be added by machine or by hand and used with any other materials that are couched onto the surface.

➤ *Try couching interesting papers, iridescent wrappings or knotted wools and other strips of torn fabric to a surface. This tends to work best on smaller quilt art pieces.*

Cross stitch This familiar stitch can take on many different uses in surface decoration. It can link two sections of fabric together as well as bringing extra colour and design. In a quilt top, it could be used as a basting stitch along with other simple variations used to stitch layers together. Another version is the herringbone stitch, which was traditionally used in world textiles to join thick materials, such as animal skins, or bark cloth.

Seeding Random stitches of this type, worked by hand, are often seen in contemporary quilts. They can add dimension and shading, create movement across the surface, fill in colour and blend areas of contrast and pattern. Seeding can also represent a visual mark when materials such as metal or lustre threads are used.

➤ *Consider creating a small quilted wall-hanging that could incorporate some extra hand stitches. Use something created in a design class in an earlier chapter.*

a *French knot*
b *Couching stitch*
c *Fly stitch*
d *Feather stitch*
e *Back stitch*
f *Herringbone*
g *Knotting strands together*

Machine embroidery

In the last 15 years, the use of machine quilting has increased to such an extent that in many modern quilt art pieces it is hard to find completely hand-quilted work. This reflects our busy lives and the facility we have to move from large bed quilts (often quilted using a long arm) to smaller gallery art quilts. The emphasis on more artistic and emotive themes means we can be working on several pieces at the same time, so the sewing machine has truly become a valuable tool.

Modern machines offer the possibility of creating a great number of stitch patterns and motifs, and some provide the facility for computer-aided design.

Back to basics

It is essential to know your machine if you are to get the best results possible. Experiment and play are important starting points, especially if you are working through surfaces you have never used before. These stitch samples will provide a great place to try different techniques, first by machine and then with added hand stitches. You don't need the fanciest or most expensive machine to get great results, but you need the essential darning foot (quilting or embroidery foot) for free-motion stitching, the ability to drop the feed dogs, variable top and bobbin tension and a simple selection of stitches that includes zigzag. Another good feature would be a 'needle down' facility, or perhaps different choices of speed.

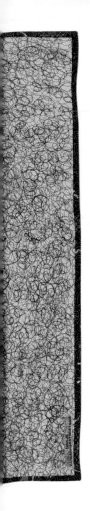

Far left: **Le Numero** *(Dirkje van der Horst Beetsma, Netherlands). This dimensional quilt includes stiffened pleats and intense machine quilting.*

Opposite page, bottom: **Grafitti No. 1: The Warrior (detail)** *(Bente Vold Klausen, Norway). Machine quilting becomes a continuous line moving across the surface.*

Left: **Graveyard** *(Bente Vold Klausen, Norway). Painted and dyed fabric with acrylic print marks. Below:* **Sampler Quilt** *(detail) (Sara Impey, UK). Machine quilting adds depth and transparency.*

Wadding

Just as the size of the quilts we make varies so much, so too do the types of wadding (batting) available. Thinner, firmer ones will be good for smaller quilted samples, while a higher loft allows for dimension in wall hangings. It is always best to experiment with something you prefer, and this will depend on the type of fabric you like to work with. Natural waddings may be more suitable for bed quilts or hangings that are hand quilted, while man-made fibres can be suitable for art quilts. Since I work with acrylic painted onto cotton as well as transferred imagery, both of which are relatively thick surfaces, my choice of wadding is a high-loft polyester wadding.

Machine threads

Again, there are so many threads to choose from these days that it becomes a matter of preference, as well as attention to the kind of mark you want to make or the thickness and type of surface you are working with. Plastics, paper and acrylic on cotton, as well as some transferred images, will require a smaller needle size (so the holes pierced are not too visible), which can dictate the type of machine-embroidery threads used.

For colour and added dimension, try using some of the wonderful variegated threads that are available. Thicker types, such as No. 30, can also be used for hand stitching and work especially well with the seeding stitch.

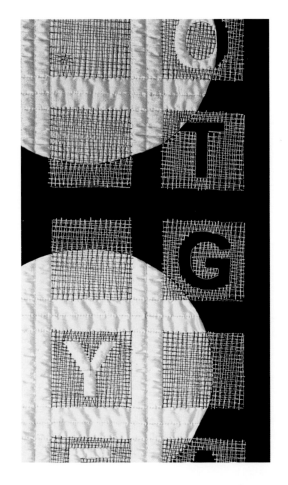

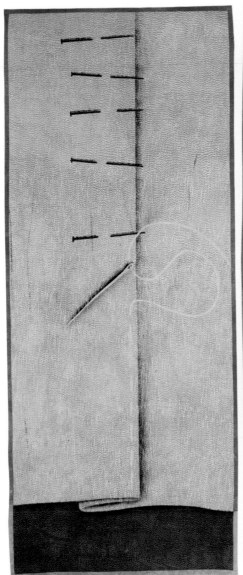
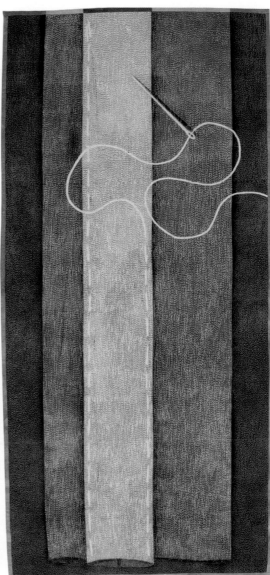

Drawing with line

Machine quilting first became established when it mimicked the kind of contour or pattern stitch that was familiar from hand quilting. Now, in the world of contemporary quilt art, the machine-quilted line can make a statement on its own. Often worked in a contrast colour, with a variety of stitch thicknesses, these lines have another design agenda on the surface. This can be the most exciting part of the quilting process. For me, creating and painting fabrics, then piecing or applying them in layers is only the beginning. The surface comes alive when the layers are machine quilted. The play of light and shade is the real dynamic element in the end.

➤ *Consider doing warm-up exercises with the machine, freely moving the needle to your favourite music.*

➤ *Try choosing some meaningful words at random and mimicking the feeling in machine stitching on a sample piece.*

➤ *Look at a picture and try to draw it with line directly onto fabric. Do not draw the image first – just have some fun.*

Opposite page: **Limited Edition** *(Bethan Ash, UK). The juxtaposition of cut pieces in this quilt may be abstract, but the design is deliberate, with strong attention to colour, shape and pattern and a balanced composition. Above left and right:* **Pleat In Yellow** *and* **Double Fold in Pink** *(Bobby Britnell, UK). Studies in pleats and folds in garment-making.*

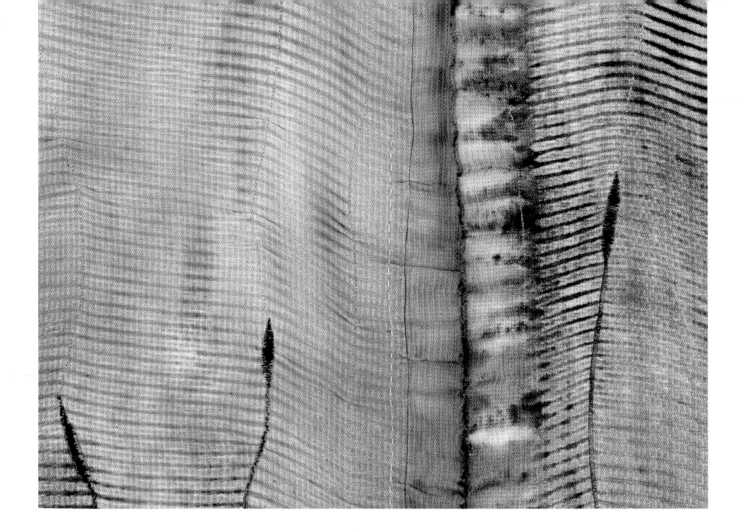

Zigzag and satin stitch

This is a popular stitch for quilters, as it can act as an edging through layers, be used to appliqué one piece to another, become a joining stitch, or be an intense bullet-style stitch, used for decoration.

➤ *Consider using 'bullets' – a tight section of satin stitch forming a square shape – in random places on the quilted surface. Bullets really need to be placed in a random, natural way, and not resemble a pattern. This extra detail will help move the eye across the surface of the work.*

Bobbin-fill techniques

For some time now, quilters have been using interesting thicker threads in the machine bobbin as a decorative statement for their art quilts. The top thread is a regular machine-quilting weight – 40/50 – and stitching is from the back of the quilt, so a raised, twisted or metallic thread will appear on top.

Decoration and embellishment

Depending on the theme, extra decoration could accent a piece of work. If world textiles are the subject, then techniques such as shisha glass detail or simple tassels might be used. Glass, plastic, wood, or hand-made beads and buttons could create impact on the surface, giving extra texture.

Opposite page: **Haliburton Highlands** *(Sandra Meech). From the Near North series Photo imagery with organza and painted and quilted fabric. Working in black and white emphasized the haunting quality of the woodland images Above:* **Clonrush** *(detail) (Ann Fahy, Ireland).*

Materials

Here are a few suggestions for materials you could use:

➤ Black-and-white images, colour copies, painted copies, textured paper, items from magazines and newspapers

➤ Handmade or other interesting papers

➤ Wool, net, acrylic and fabric-painted cloth, Bali and batik prints

➤ Your own hand-dyed cotton or transfer-dyed fabrics

➤ Tyvek or even Wireform, for three-dimensional pages or covers

➤ Embroidery threads in a variety of colours, perlé and stranded cottons, wools, twists, raffia, for hand stitching

➤ Embellishment, beads and buttons

In addition you will need:

➤ Thin wadding, heaviest and thinner weights of interfacing (Vilene or Pellon products or similar)

➤ Bondaweb (Wonder Under) or similar iron-on adhesive material; 405 fabric adhesive spray

➤ Sewing machine and embroidery threads and selection of needles

➤ Beads or metallic threads

➤ Cutting board, ruler, rotary cutting tool, paper and fabric scissors

➤ Glue stick

For the textured book cover:

➤ An ordinary bound or spiral-bound book of your choice

For the Japanese stab-bound book:

➤ Thin card – four pieces the same size as the book you are creating

➤ Additional fabric for the inside covers

➤ Binder clips to keep pages in place

➤ An awl or hole-piercing device, toothpicks, a large chenille needle

➤ Extra interesting cord/ribbon for tying

Design class – sumptuous stitch books

Creating your own personal embellished books can be an expressive statement, a unique way of exploring new sewing techniques or using a wealth of interesting mixed-media materials that you may not wish to incorporate into an art quilt. This design class is in two parts:

1. **A traditional embellished book cover** – the example chosen measures 17.5cm x 12.5cm (7 x 5in), but the instructions can be adapted to any size. This cover will fit bound books, diaries, address books and so on, as well as spiral sketchbooks and plastic ring-bound books.
2. **A Japanese stab-bound book** – this is a simple bound book, the same size as the one above, which again can be adapted to any size. Decorative embellished machined and hand-stitched covers will make this special.

Textured book cover

1. Measure the surface that will be covered by measuring the book closed and measuring from edge to edge, adding 10cm (4in) to the width (allows for two 5cm/2in inside flaps). Create a bigger surface area than you need.
2. Create a collage of fabric and paper to cover the surface – perhaps a composition exercise. Remember that the front should include the most interesting design treatment – when lying flat, this is on the right-hand side. Prepare for stitching by pinning the surface onto thin wadding with a heavy interfacing base (fig a).
3. Move across the surface with a free and interpretative machine quilting style – keep stitching threads simple as they will also be used for the satin-stitch edging.
4. Some hand stitching or other embellishments (wire, metal, couching) could be used to accent certain areas at this time.

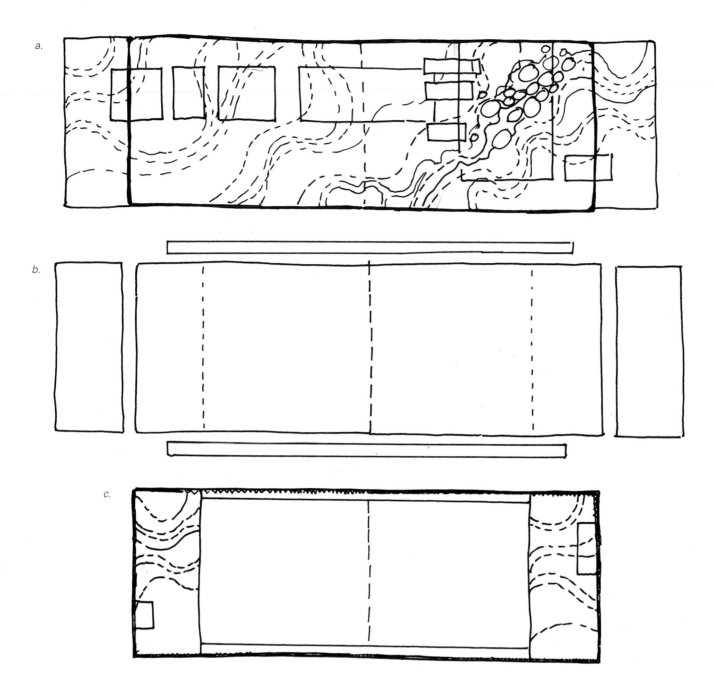

a.

b.

c.

5. Measure and cut out accurately the width and length of the cover (the book needs to be closed to calculate this), adding at least 6mm (¼in) all the way around. You should also have allowed for the two inside cover flaps (see fig *b*, above).

6. A thin stabilizing band will help maintain the structure at the top and bottom of the cover. Cut this from Bondaweb (Wonder Under) or similar.

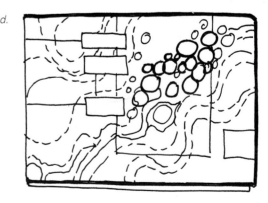

d.

Satin stitch edge

7. Beginning in the middle at the top or bottom edge and working with the wrong side of the cover upwards, the stabilizing band in place and side flaps turned in, begin sewing with a wide zigzag stitch. Work out to one side and then the other, and then complete the other edge (see fig *c*, above).

a.

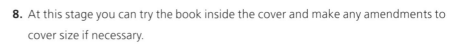

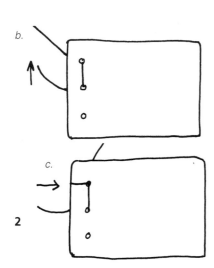

b.

c.

2

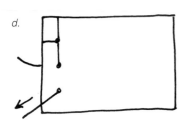

d.

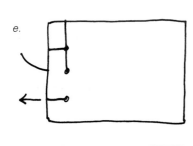

e.

f.

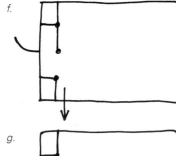

g.

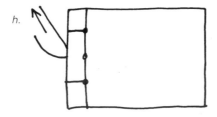

h.

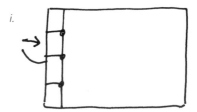

i.

8. At this stage you can try the book inside the cover and make any amendments to cover size if necessary.

9. Snip the corners and begin a tight satin stitch (at least 3mm/⅛in wide), working with the right side upwards and starting from the spine. Be careful when going around the corners to make sure that the stitching is smooth and as even as possible (see fig *d* on page 115).

The finished cover may be a little stiff at first, but will become more flexible with use.

A Japanese stab-bound book

Embellished collage and compositional exercises could make an inspired cover for a Japanese stab-bound book. Simple Japanese stab bindings have been included to make this wonderful treasured book.

1. You will have four cover pieces altogether: two outer cover pieces and two inside covers.

2. Stitch one large piece of embellished fabric, measuring at least 20 x 28cm (8 x 11in) for each top cover. Consider using interesting commercial fabrics, and Bali or batik designs as a base for more embellishment. Have fun couching wools or incorporate transfer-dyed fabrics. This top cover will form a sandwich with a middle of thin wadding and backing of firm interfacing (see fig *a*).

3. The inside covers, which are the same size as the outer cover, will be a plain fabric – perhaps a simple batik or hand-dyed piece of fabric – bonded onto firm interfacing such as Bondaweb (Wonder Under).

4. Trim all pieces to measure 17.5 x 12.5cm (7 x 5in).

5. Place one outside and one inside cover together for the front; repeat for the back. Satin stitch (a wide stitch first, then a tighter final one) around three sides of each pair of covers, leaving a short side open where it will be bound.

6. Cut four pieces of card, each 13.7 x 10cm (5½ x 4in). Place one piece in the front cover and three in the back cover. Push them to the outer edge to allow for the cover to open easily on the left.

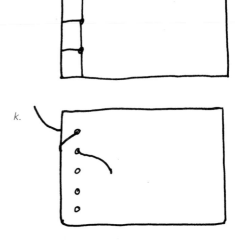

7. Satin stitch the last edge of both the front and back covers.

8. Compile the material for your pages – paper, fabric, sewn collage material and anything you choose, trimming them to a slightly smaller measure than the covers, say 17.7 x 11.2cm (6½ x 4½in).

9. Measure where the holes should be. This can be worked out on a piece of card ahead of time. Odd numbers work best. Using clamps to keep the book together, take an awl or piercing tool (one that will give a hole measuring at least 1.5mm/¹⁄₁₆in in diameter). Break a toothpick in half and place into the hole to secure the book.

10. Decide on a simple stab binding. Thread the chenille needle with ribbon, raffia, or interesting wool and cord and have fun.

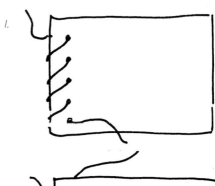

The best way to try some different stab bindings is to practise on some card or spare bits of painted papers first. Some examples are shown here: figs *b–j* show a conventional stab binding, and figs *k–m* show another simple alternative. Fig *n* shows binding with a twig or stick, and fig *o* shows the finished cover.

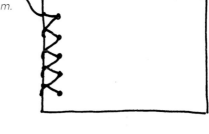

Below: Japanese stab-bound book covers.

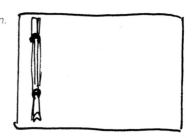

Right and below: **Thelon** *(Sandra Meech). This piece was part of a collaboration with contemporary jewellers in the Fusion touring exhibition. The pendant by Georgina Taylor inspired this quilt.*

Taking your work further

It doesn't matter how long you have been quilting or what aspect of contemporary quilting you identify with, there is no reason why you can't adopt a professional approach to your work. By planning themes and more fully researching them, you will gain richer satisfaction and build more confidence along the way.

There will doubtless be times when either distractions interrupt your commitment or everyday life makes it more difficult to focus on the deadlines for an exhibition. This is when sketchbook ideas could be developed and small experimental samples explored, which, when time permits, may be developed into a series of work. Perhaps teaching workshops or lecturing to groups may be part of the next step. Or you may want to start a business related to contemporary quilting, designing patterns or promoting your work commercially. You may already be affiliated to a national guild as well as a local group, but perhaps it may be time to consider a personal website, as the internet has become such a wonderful tool for communication.

Now is the time to ask yourself some important questions about your work and yourself as a textile artist. Where do I see myself in five years? What aspects of this field really excite me? Do I need more direction, focus and experimentation? Do I need to concentrate on a certain style of work, a concentrated theme, or a new technique that will distinguish my work? We all ask these questions frequently and perhaps it is time to think of some answers that might make the future journey more exciting.

Above: **Lille Wall** (*Sandra Meech*). *The original poster image shown on page 10, enhanced in Photoshop.*

Below left and right: **Ritual Cloth III** *and* **Ritual Cloth I** (*Joanie San Chirico, USA*). *Digitally printed cloth from acrylic paintings.*

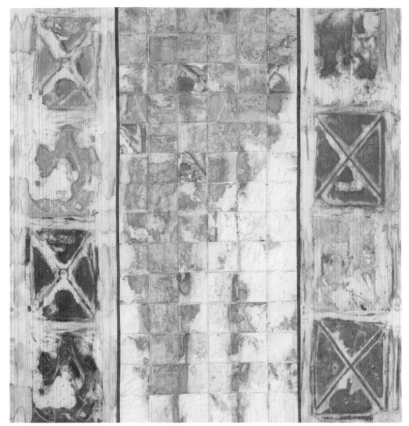

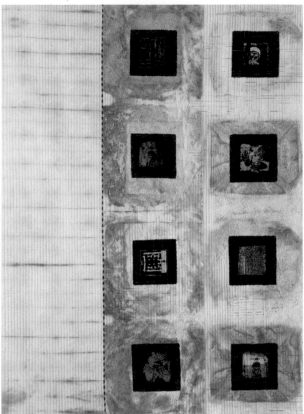

Above left: **Imprints of Time 4**. *Above right:* **Rust, Secrets from the Desert** *(Charlotte Yde, Denmark).* This series is inspired by frescoes excavated in the Nubian desert.

Working in series

Establishing a theme that will keep you inspired for some time makes your creative journey a very fulfilling one. All too often we respond to exhibition themes or competitions with deadlines, but however important it is to get our work out there to the viewing public, it is equally important to be satisfied and fulfilled in what we do. The textile artist who has a body of work based on a specific subject can become totally involved in every aspect of it, taking inspiration from everyday events that may impact this theme. There are many ways in which working in series can be beneficial. It can offer a textile artist the following advantages:

➤ *The freedom to create a series of similar-sized pieces that could eventually become a solo exhibition.*

➤ *The ability to move from different disciplines in stitched textiles – create small embroidered or embellished works one time and large dynamic wall quilts another – all on the same theme.*

➤ *The chance to explore different techniques each time but have a common theme or colour uniting all the work, thus staying true to the integrity of the theme.*

➤ *The opportunity to work a large design that is broken into different parts. The integral pieces have to work as one when hanging together, but can also be sufficiently well designed to stand alone.*

Above: **Rust Studies** *(Charlotte Yde, Denmark). Installation pieces.*

120

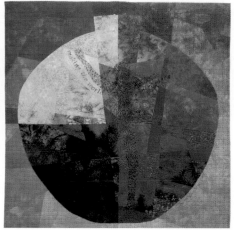

Exhibiting in groups

It is always easier to find venues, local or otherwise, when you have group support. All members need to be dedicated to a common aim and all committed to exhibiting. They must all be prepared to take on the tasks involved:

➤ *Advertising through magazines and 'what's on' diaries.*
➤ *Arranging for general publicity (posters, private view invitations).*
➤ *Creating a show catalogue of work.*
➤ *Planning 'meet the artist' events.*
➤ *Keeping a website up and running to advertise dates and information.*
➤ *Being available, if necessary, to put up and take quilts down, and for stewarding during the exhibition.*

It seems like a tall order, but professional groups are used to doing this every time they exhibit. There is also the work that is done before the venue is found, which includes finding potential galleries, gathering curator contact details and creating promotional material (CDs or postcard and information packs). It all sounds overwhelming, but it is wonderful experience to have before you may tackle your own solo exhibition.

Above: **Making the World a Safer Place**
(Susan Denton, UK). These three 145 x 145cm (57 x 57in) pieces make a powerful and dramatic series of work.

Below: **Souvenirs 7–9, Nike Series**
(Charlotte Yde, Denmark). A series based on lost cultures, personal travel and Greek and Roman influences in Scandinavia and the rest of Europe.

Installation and dimensional work

Most contemporary quilters still think in conventional layers and many find it difficult to view quilts as anything other than wall hangings. These are exciting and diverse times and many textile artists are now also working in mixed media, exploring different dimensions and structures, but all with layers of one type or another. In quilt art terms, installations are pieces that stand alone and can be viewed from all sides. Also included in this category are wall hangings that overlay one another, those that are fixed to a wall but are distinctly 3-dimensional, or work that is suspended from the ceiling. Many of these concepts need a contemporary gallery if they are to be displayed to their best advantage. Conventional quilt exhibition display stands have their limitations.

In a public gallery, almost anything is possible. Here are some of the options:

➤ *A series of pieces that stand in front of each other, but are wall-mounted. These could be sheer or have a cut-away quality to them.*

➤ *A piece that is singular and wall-mounted that depends on light and cast shadow for interesting effects.*

➤ *A structure that is totally three-dimensional, which you can completely walk around. Considerations for weight and transportation would have to be made if the piece is meant to tour. Smaller sculptural textile pieces can be displayed on a plinth or in a display case, which can be very effective.*

➤ *Working in a smaller space that allows for flexibility in the way work is displayed. Small quilted mixed-media installations, creative clothing or contemporary doll and figure art could be included. There is such a wonderful 'cross-over' of fibre disciplines available to us.*

Opposite page: **Talisman Towers** *(Linda Kemshall, UK). Installation in paper and stitch.*

Left: **Martial Arts Momma** *(Margi Hennen, Canada). Art doll.*

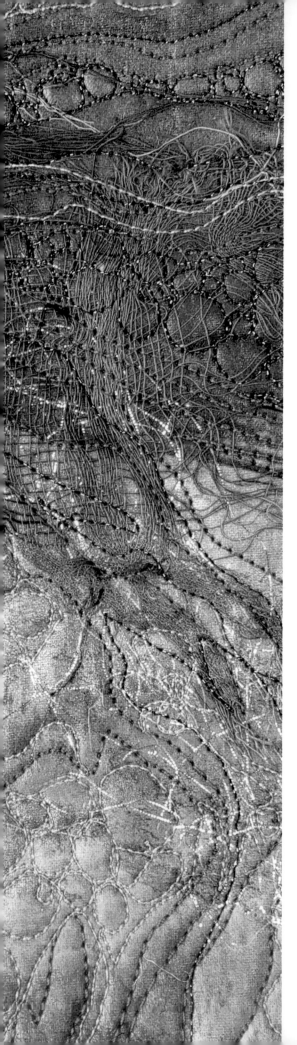

The artist statement

When textile artists are promoting themselves, they need to listen to their 'inner voice' and decide exactly what they want to say. More commercial endeavours, such as the design of patterns and kits, or the supply of hand-dyed fabrics or stitch and surface design products, may require a more snappy presentation. For the individual creative artist, who wants to exhibit, work to commission and create work to a theme, a more simplified approach would work.

A personal statement on the style and theme of work is an essential first step. Again, it comes easier if there is hidden meaning to the work being done. It is not necessary to take a cerebral approach, but taking a deeper, sensitive approach to your work will pay dividends. Certainly in juried exhibitions, a well-constructed artist's statement – one that informs on several layers of meaning – will be considered more seriously. The most important thing is that the work is interesting, and well designed and executed, but insightful pieces will always win that prestigious place.

Personal promotion

Before the World Wide Web, life was simpler and textile artists managed with business cards, postcards to show their work with contact details on the back and 'artist profile' information about any exhibition in which they were included. This is still a very valuable approach, but it has been superseded to some extent by the personal website. Email has also become an important tool for world-wide communication. Digital images are transferred through cyberspace, and it is now possible, with high-resolution photographs, to send one's work on CD anywhere.

Website design can be expensive, and I know from personal experience that it takes time and expertise to create one. It may be necessary to have one in order to get ahead, and it is seductive to dip into many wonderful sites and want the same kind of profile. I certainly believe that, at a certain level, a personal website is a valuable tool, whether you just want to promote your work in the public sector, to sell pieces or to advertise your teaching, lecturing and diary programme.

Even the personal diary or 'blog' sites that are popular can be an interesting and informative way of keeping in touch with other art quilters around the globe. Perhaps this isn't for everyone, but it is a large part of a professional quilt artist's world.

Left: **Winter Sun (detail)** *(Sandra Meech). A small experimental stitched piece which blends photo-transferred imagery, quilting through layers and embellishment by hand and machine.*

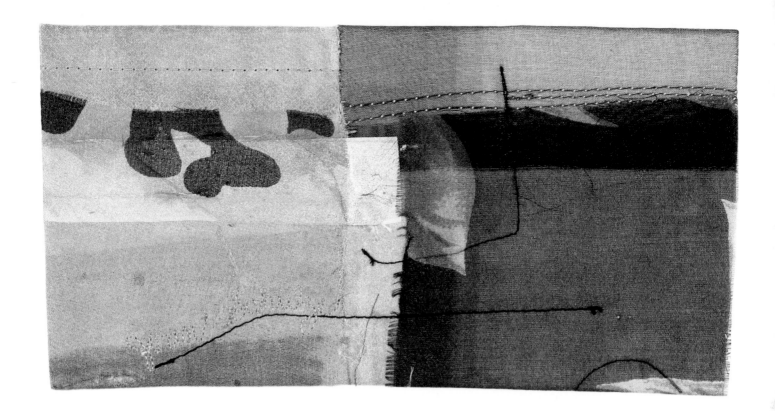

In Conclusion

With aspects of quiltmaking, embroidery and other forms of textile art merging into a more inclusive world of stitched textiles, these are exciting times. No longer do quilters have to make quilts simply for beds and warmth, or embroiderers confine themselves to small pieces of handwork. Both types of artist can make creative, innovative pieces that are full of personal expression. What's more, contemporary textile art doesn't always have to be worthy, political or full of depth and insight: artists can also celebrate humour, whim, glitz and glamour. The important thing to remember is that all artists have the ability to reach their own creative potential, explore new inspiration in the world around them and express themselves in fabric and stitch with more confidence than ever before.

If you take yourself seriously as a quilt or stitched textile artist, you will have taken a first step on the road to achieving the level of creativity you want for yourself. Follow through with the suggestions, techniques and classes in this book and you will be well on the way to achieving your own personal potential – with, I hope, plenty of exciting challenges and fun as you go.

Above: **A Flower, A Leaf** *(Joan Schulz, USA).*
A treasured piece from an artist whose work I have admired for many years.

Glossary

Acrylic paint used on untreated cotton can give interesting effects which can later inspire machine stitch. Watering it down will allow for easy stitching or make it suitable for applying on the glue side of Bondaweb or Wonder Under for interesting effects. Let the Bondaweb dry thoroughly, then iron face down onto cotton and peel off the paper backing to reveal a natural, organic-looking pattern (please note this cannot be ironed).

Baking parchment, also known as silicone paper, can be used to protect the iron from adhesive materials such as Bondaweb (Wonder Under), bonding powder, acrylic paint, plastics and other man-made fibres that could spoil the surface of the iron. White or beige opaque Teflon sheets are a good alternative.

Bondaweb (Wonder Under) is an adhesive fabric that comes both in sheets and by the roll. It is used for bonding fabrics together. Its use will stiffen fabric so machine quilting rather than hand stitch is necessary.

Bonding powder is a fine, granular form of adhesive used with wool, threads, net, sheers etc to create surface embellishment. Parchment is used to protect the iron.

Brusho and Koh-I-noor are water-based dyes used for painting paper. Brusho comes in powder form (a rounded teaspoon mixed with 590ml (2 oz) water makes a strong solution). Koh-I-noor is a palette of 12 waterproof dye colours which is perfect for travelling. Wax resist and bleach work well with these dyes.

Collage Generally, collage is considered as a composition of materials and objects pasted on a surface, often developed with unifying colour and line. In today's stitched textiles the term can apply to pasted, glued or overlaid materials that could include paper, fabric, plastics, sheers, net, wire, beads and other materials held together and embellished further with stitch.

Colour Understanding the rules of colour is very important for textile artists. The colour wheel consists of the primary colours red, yellow and blue, and the secondary colours orange (yellow/red mix), green (yellow/blue mix) and purple (blue/red mix). Next are the tertiary colours: yellow/orange, orange, orange/red, red, red/purple, purple, purple/blue… and so on around the wheel. Combinations of complementary colours, from opposite sides of the colour wheel, are seen everywhere in nature – red and green, orange and blue and purple and yellow. Analagous colours make powerful combinations: try taking three or four colours from one side of the wheel (for example green, turquoise and blue) with a touch of the colour opposite (in this case, orange).

The rule of thirds is the simplified version of the golden section rectangle, a graphic interpretation of the Fibonacci number sequence. Fibonacci, a thirteenth-century mathematician, arrived at a sequence in which each number is the sum of the previous two: 0+1=1, 1+1=2 2+1=3 3+2=5, 5+3=8, 8+5=13, 13+8=21 and so on…. . This pattern is found everywhere in nature, for example in the pattern of the veins of a leaf, the spiral in a conch shell or the seeds of a sunflower. Keep these design rules in mind when you find the focal point or area of interest in your textile pieces.

Embellishment can be created with any number of materials. A favourite is Angelina fibres, iridescent paper waste which can be heat-melted (with an iron) with other fibres for surface embellishment. Dyed scrim (muslin) with an open weave can be manipulated and used effectively when stiffened with PVA (craft) glue. Beads, buttons, wire, sequins or world-textile materials such as shisha or mirrored glass, braids, or tassels, are all finding their way into contemporary quilts.

Freezer paper is a silicone-based paper used to prevent condensation in frozen food products and is ironed onto fabric to stabilize it for painting, stencilling, stamping or photo-transfer techniques.

Health and safety is mentioned throughout the book, but is an important issue. Any dye powders, including Procion, disperse transfer and Brusho can be airborne when mixed, so a mask is essential. Heat transfer onto polyester materials also can be slightly toxic, which could affect those with respiratory weaknesses. Make sure you work in a well-ventilated space.

Interfacing is used mainly in the clothing industry but can be used in textile art as a thin wadding (batting) to create the necessary backing layer for mixed materials including paper, plastics and fabric. Very stiff interfacings like craft or pelmet Vilene (Pellon) give a firm backing to wall-hung pieces, boxes and book covers.

Photographic transfer methods are used with increasing popularity in contemporary quilts. Today, there are many methods to choose from. In my own work, I use an acrylic medium called 'Picture This' by Plaid. The medium is spread thinly over the surface of a laser-jet colour copy with a sponge applicator (the image is in reverse), and laid face down onto prepared cotton (pre-washed white cotton ironed onto freezer paper). The resulting image 'sandwich' is placed in a warm, dry place for 24 hours, the freezer paper is removed (it can be used again) and the image is soaked for several minutes in tepid water. The paper backing is then rubbed off with a sponge. Around 90% of the backing usually comes off the first time, but when dry a film of paper will remain which has to be gently removed by rubbing with the sponge again. This plasticized fabric cannot be ironed and any holes made on the surface are permanent. Nevertheless the results can be very realistic and with machine quilting through a high-loft wadding (batting), interesting dimension can be achieved. Bubble Jet Set 2000 is another liquid medium which allows cotton, when ironed onto freezer paper and trimmed precisely to size, to become a surface that can be fed into a household ink-jet printer. This means that photographs and images originally created on a computer can be transferred onto cloth with pleasing results. Laser Trans or similar transfer papers are another popular method. With computer-generated images (also in reverse or mirrored) you can print in colour directly onto ink-jet paper and, with a hot dry iron, transfer the image onto cotton. Professional digital printing is also a possibility: images can be computer-manipulated and emailed to printing houses that can provide enlargements on cotton up to 152cm (60in) wide. Other methods, old and new, can be found in numerous books on image transfer. Photo imagery in contemporary quilts is here to stay.

Plastics are frequently used in contemporary quilts. Begin by experimenting with plastics that are easily available. Bubble wrap and plastic ring-binder sleeves work well, as do some clear plastic food wraps. Beware of mildly toxic fumes when heating and burning plastics and protect your iron with parchment or a similar material. More professional laminating plastics may be worth considering.

Transfer dyeing originated as a commercial process for heat-printing motifs and pattern onto poly-cotton fabric in the soft furnishing industry (bedlinen, duvet covers). For several years, stitched textile artists have used transfer-dye methods to create interesting surfaces on cloth for hand and machine stitching. Once only available in pre-mixed bottles of colour (such as Deka transfer paints), disperse transfer dyes are now available in powder form (1 rounded teaspoon with 590ml (2 oz) water makes a strong mix). Painted onto thin, hard paper – artists' layout paper works well as it has a hard surface – and

ironing onto fabrics can achieve interesting results. You could try resists (perhaps candle wax or oil pastels) first, then scrunch the paper (which gives marbled patterns when ironed) and let dry thoroughly. Fabrics can include 100% polyester materials such as interfacings, curtain net, sheers or linings – a blend of poly-cotton and even tightly woven cotton will take the transfer dye. Experiment with weaving, cutting shapes, or overlapping papers for interesting results and remember you can get

up to 3 or 4 prints from each, and afterwards the paper itself is interesting to use in mixed-media stitch collage.

Wireform is a wire mesh demonstrated in the Design Class on page 96. It is fine enough to use as a fourth layer in a contemporary quilt, but strong enough to hold its shape after manipulation. Copper wire is softer, but all thin mesh can dull machine needles quickly.

Bibliography

Atkinson, Jennifer L. *Collage Art: A Step-by Step Guide and Showcase*. Rockport, 2004

Beam, Mary Todd. *Celebrate your Creative Self*. North Light Books, 2001

Beaney, Jan and Littlejohn, Jean. *A Sketch in Time*. Double Trouble Enterprises, 2003

Brommer, Gerald. *Collage Techniques*. Watson–Guptill Publications, 1994

Burbidge, Pauline. *Quilt Studio*. The Quilt Digest Press, 2000

Diehn, Gwen. *The Decorated Page*. Lark Books, 2003

Dunwold, June. *Complex Cloth*. Fibre Studio Press, 1996

Faimon, Peg and Weigand, John. *The Nature of Design*. HOW Design Books, 2004

Genders, Carolyn. *Sources of Inspiration*. A & C Black, 2004

Gillow, John and Sentence, Bryan. *World Textiles*. Thames & Hudson, 2004

Green, Jean Drysdale. *Arteffects*. Watson Guptill Publications, 1993

Greenlees, Kay. *Creating Sketchbooks for Embroiderers and Textile Artists*. Batsford, 2005

Grey, Maggie and Wild, Jane. *Paper, Metal and Stitch*. Batsford, 2004

Grey, Maggie. *Raising the Surface with Machine Embroidery*. Batsford, 2003

Issett Ruth: *Colour on Paper and Fabric*. Batsford, 2000

Issett, Ruth. *Glorious Papers*. Batsford, 2001

Jerstorp, Karin and Kohlmark, Eva. *The Textile Design Book*. A & C Black, 1989

LaPlantz, Shereen. *Cover to Cover*. Lark Books, 1998.

Laury, Jean Ray. *Imagery on Fabric*. C & T, 1997

Laury, Jean Ray. *The Photo Transfer Handbook*. C & T, 1999

Leland, Nita. *The Creative Artist*. North Light Books, 1993

Leland, Nita and Williams, Virginia Lee. *Creative Collage Techniques*. North Light Books, 2001

Michel, Karen. *The Complete Guide to Altered Imagery*. Quarry Books, 2005

Oei, Loan and De Kegel, Cecile. *The Elements of Design*. Thames & Hudson, 2002

Schulze, Joan. *The Art of Joan Schulze*. Custom & Limited Editions, 1999

Scott, Jac. *Textile Perspectives in Mixed Media Sculpture*. The Crowood Press, 2003

Sleigh, Mary. *African Inspirations in Embroidery*. Batsford, 2004

Springall, Diana. *Inspired to Stitch: 21 Textile Artists*. A & C Black, 2005

Taylor, Terry. *Altered Art*. Lark Books, 2005

Suppliers

UK Suppliers
• Art Van Go Tel: 01438 814946
www.artvango.co.uk
• Rainbow Silks Tel: 01494 862111
www.rainbowsilks.co.uk
• Colourcraft (Brusho paint, Disperse Transfer Dyes) Tel: 0114 242 1431
www.colourcraftltd.com
• Kemtex Colours Tel: 01257 230220
www.kemtex.co.uk
• Freudenberg Nonwovens LP (Vilene/Pellon interfacings) Tel: 01422 327900
www.nonwovens-group.com

• Whaleys (Bradford) Ltd Tel: 01274 521309
www.whaleys-bradford.ltd.uk
• The African Fabric Shop
www.africanfabric.co.uk

USA and Canada suppliers
• PRO Chemical & Dye Inc Tel: 800 228 9393
www.prochemical.com
• Dharma Trading Company Tel: 800 542 5227 www.dharmatrading.com
• Meinke Toy www.meinketoy.com
• G & S Dyes & Accessories Ltd
Tel: (416) 596 0550 www.gsdye.com

Groups
• Quilt Art (international group):
www.quiltart.org.uk
• The Quilters' Guild of the British Isles:
www.quiltersguild.org.uk
• Canadian Quilters' Association:
www.canadianquilter.com
• The Embroiderers' Guild:
www.embroiderersguild.com